HORSES AND THE
MYSTICAL PATH

HORSES AND THE MYSTICAL PATH

THE CELTIC WAY
OF EXPANDING
THE HUMAN SOUL

Adele von Rüst McCormick, Ph.D.
Marlena Deborah McCormick, Ph.D.
Thomas E. McCormick, M.D.

NEW WORLD LIBRARY
NOVATO, CALIFORNIA

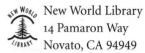
New World Library
14 Pamaron Way
Novato, CA 94949

Cover design by Mary Ann Casler
Interior design and typography by Tona Pearce Myers

Library of Congress Cataloging-in-Publication Data
McCormick, Adele von Rüst, 1929–
  Horses and the mystical path : the Celtic way of expanding the human soul / Adele von Rüst McCormick, Marlena Deborah McCormick, Thomas E. McCormick.— 1st ed.
     p.   cm.
  Includes bibliographical references and index.
  ISBN 1-57731-450-6 (hardcover : alk. paper)
  1. Horses—Religious aspects. 2. Celts—Religion. 3. Spiritual life.
I. McCormick, Marlena Deborah II. McCormick, Thomas E. III. Title.
  BV443.H6M3 2004
  202'.12—dc22   2004009010

First printing, September 2004
ISBN 1-57731-450-6

Printed in Canada on 100% postconsumer waste recycled paper

A proud member of the Green Press Initiative

Distributed to the trade by Publishers Group West

10   9   8   7   6   5   4   3   2   1

TO F.P.C. TRIANERO +,
our twenty-nine-year-old Peruvian stallion.

You renewed our faith, spirit, and soul
and awakened our inner nature
by restoring our oneness with the Cosmos.

CONTENTS

Acknowledgments

We wish to thank with great esteem our editor, Hal Zina Bennett, who understands us and our horses. It was mystical to have you aboard, Hal.

We also wish to thank our clients and fellow travelers on the path. Without you there would be no book. You were our inspiration.

Of course, we wish to let the world know how horses can heal and that their relationship with us is most precious. The chakras are always open.

We wish to thank and praise Jason Gardner, senior editor of New World Library in California. You are a gem among editors and publishers.

To Barbara Neighbors Deal, our most patient, loving, and wise agent. You are a blessing in our lives.

We thank Joseph Dial, executive director of the Mind/Science Foundation in San Antonio, Texas, who understands that one mystery only uncovers another.

Women at the Well in San Antonio, we love you all. Thank you to the Hispanic Heritage Society, who proved classical riding is in the "blood."

Our many thanks to Animal Planet and the production company Palazzina Productions. Thank you, Manon de Jong, Rene, and Pasqual, for your creative and inspiring vision.

To our friend the Buddhist monk Javier Malcolm, who has shown us there is more than one way.

Thank you to our dear friends Shelley and Jean-Philippe Giacomini, who brought us into the wonderful world of Iberian horses.

And our gratitude to our dear friend of thirty-five years, José María Poveda de Augustine, M.D., Ph.D., author of *Chamanismo: El arte natural de curar,* in Madrid, Spain.

Introduction

Traveler, your footprints
are the road, and nothing more;
traveler, there is no road,
the road is made by moving.

— Antonio Machado (1875–1939)

W hen our journey with horses and healing began, more than twenty-five years ago, we never imagined that horses would lead us down a mystical path. Nor did we foresee how valuable and enriching this experience would be, not just for us but for the hundreds of people who have participated in our Equine Experience retreats. Yet from the start, the horses we were breeding taught us the silent knowledge of who we are. They helped us cut away the chaff, the empty words and trends, and stay close to the knowledge and skills that have endured the test of time.

A cornerstone that grounded our ever-growing perceptions of the spiritual domain was our past training in analytic depth psychology. Rather than discarding what we had previously learned about working with ourselves and other people, we began to integrate and use much of our knowledge of psychology. We were not leaving our foundation behind but building upon it. We discovered that if we were to be effective in our work, we needed to use both psychology and spirituality.

We stood at a crossroads between psychology and religion, and we could see that these two disciplines, which had been at cross-purposes for years, needed to be reintegrated. One lost its potency without the other. Through the horses, we started reconciling these two approaches, moving increasingly toward the psychospiritual. Psychology without spirituality leads to one set of problems, while spirituality without psychology leads to another.

We were reminded again that the human psyche is the entry point to the creative force within each of us. If we fail to know this inner self, our spiritual and creative resources remain inaccessible. Meditation, spiritual study, chanting, and prayer are no substitutes for self-examination. Every mystical tradition requires inner exploration, which brings greater depth and substance to the person who is developing spiritually.

We found, over time, that in order for the mystical quest with a horse to remain progressive instead of regressive, we had to learn to recognize our juvenile fantasies and wishes as they emerged. And emerge they will in this work with horses. Once we recognize these early needs, we can redirect our attention away from feeding them and toward unlocking our imagination. Imagination, according to famous psychiatrist D. W. Winnicott, is entering the experience and situation of another being without seeking selfish gratification, pleasure, or notoriety. The imagination is the key to a vibrant life. Since we can become ill through the mind, we can also become healthy by exercising the imagination. By contrast, fixation on infantile fantasies invariably leads to disappointment, disillusionment, and despair. As we searched for different paradigms that could spark the human imagination and inspire self-education, we reached back into the annals of history.

In time, we found ourselves on a mysterious and intriguing wisdom pilgrimage. Each encounter brought us, and the people we worked with, closer to a new way of being. On the road from India to Santiago de Compostela to southern Spain and Morocco, we followed the age-old relationship between horses and humans.

Soon, we came into contact with a seemingly timeless and eternal group of horsemen and -women who followed a mystical path and embraced many of the same philosophies we held. These men and women intentionally befriended the horse to cultivate the human heart and soul, reduce the Ego, and live on the very cusp of the seen and unseen worlds. This adventurous place is the location of divine mystery; both inside and outside us, it's where life is vibrant and created anew. It is a locale of discovery where we find ourselves in the presence of the Invisible One.

The Celtic Connection

Through some very strange and serendipitous encounters, we discovered that it was the ancient Celtic people who gave birth to this prototypical psychospiritual nature paradigm. The Celtic people used communing with horses for human development, awareness, and spiritual growth. Horses, if given the opportunity, would highlight the defenses that stood in each human being's way, thrusting people into ever-increasing levels of self-awareness. By accepting the equine reaction, a person would commune with the heart of nature while also questioning personal habits and beliefs. Dialoguing with a horse was also a vehicle for intensifying intimacy with God, for the Celts believed the Infinite One speaks through all Creation. We've found these things to be true. Kinship with animals brings us into direct contact with our cosmic origins, divine attributes, and sacred resources. Merging with horses, as long as it is not for self-aggrandizement, animates the human spirit and furnishes it with boundless energy.

In the Celtic world, the mind (as distinct from the brain) is also a mystical faculty for creating; it is capable of basking in the mysteries, if we can let go of our material needs and return to nature. These ancient methods and practices, themselves the early roots of Western spirituality, spark this letting go, a process that brings unparalleled meaning and richness.

In this book we explore many aspects of Celtic spirituality: specifically the unusual, longstanding, and integrated Celtic understanding of nature, mysticism, and personal development. The Celts were uniquely inclusive, blending the spirituality of East and West. At one time this ancient group of horse-loving people spread their philosophies around the globe. Recent evidence from archaeologists places these ancient tribes with their horses on the Silk Road, near the Gobi Desert, approximately seven thousand years ago. Evidence of their civilization as late as 500 B.C. has also been discovered across Western Europe. They were in Asia Minor, and they were known to have settlements in the Middle East, as evidenced by St. Paul's letter to the Galatians in the Bible. They were also discovered in the deserts of the Middle East, learning from the Desert Mothers and Fathers of early Christianity around A.D. 300 to 400.

What is so unique about the ancient Celts is that, although they were tribal, anyone who embraced their wisdom, ideals, and virtues was adopted as a kinsman, including creatures. Moreover, during their travels the Celts not only influenced other cultures but were affected by them as well, fostering an open give-and-take attitude. Since they loved and incorporated many of the beliefs and customs of other peoples, the Celtic mind and heart remained flexible and receptive. Even today, if one has an affinity toward the Celtic Way, one is indeed a Celt. In essence, we are all Celts if we choose to be.

Celtic spirituality became a focus on our path, a way to rediscover the God of Creation and bring love and forgiveness back into being. It was a way to see ecology as a truly sacred task. We discovered that by revealing their hearts and minds, horses help us connect to the Divine, the very heart of the Cosmos.

You will find many stories in this book; some will make you laugh, and some will make you cry. Learning about people's deep connection with horses teaches us how to best unleash the power of grace, creativity, and love in our own lives, and it helps us understand what stands in the way of our success and creativity. The stories help reveal how being with horses within this Celtic model can unlock our inner talents and remove blocks. By these intimate encounters in the animal realm, humans regain meaning and quality in their lives and learn to conduct themselves in sensitive and bold ways. By reestablishing our cosmic connections and brotherhood, and by staying rooted in the divine ecosystem that is our universe, we learn to extract our inner toxins and unearth a gold mine of human resources.

Wisdom is in nature, including our own human nature, and there are amazing lessons to be learned. A quote from the Holy Koran articulates nature's role in our spirituality: "There are signs for believers in the heavens and the earth. And for people who have firm faith, there are signs in our own creation and in that of all living creatures." In this book, we explore how horses bring humans to this kind of bold truth.

Horses inspire us, as do soaring cathedrals, sacred sites, and high crosses. When our hearts turn toward these magnificent creatures with selfless love, our minds become still. We are captivated by their grandeur, and simultaneously reminded that with God's spirit we are full. In those moments we grow closer to God because we experience beauty. "Beauty is where 'you' are not. The essence of beauty is the absence of the self."[1]

On this journey, we learn from our interactions with the horse and from our reflections to find a spirit of unity and beauty in everything we do. By mastering the art of unity, we find that peace that is beyond understanding, that is in simply seeing *what is*. Sufi mystic Ibn Al' Arabi illuminates what occurs when this level of awareness and expanse of consciousness are reached: "The eye that sees me, sees itself."

Since we will be taking you into a world that is invisible, you must learn to trust that which you cannot see, touch, or feel. The heart is the center and the focus of this creative spiritual energy — or *theophanic energy,* the energy released when we immerse ourselves in the manifestations of God in nature — and the imagination is its organ, its vehicle of creating. "If he has given us life and existence by his being, I also give him life by knowing him in my heart," says Henry Corbin, describing the philosophy of Al' Arabi.[2]

We will take you on our road, an adventure into the heart of nature, where the wild ones reside. So enjoy the ride, enjoy the read. You will find yourself in a most exciting world as we learn to open ourselves to ourselves and to the One.

Ultimately, we will reveal to you what can happen when you stand before a horse in complete and utter humility, full of respect and wonder, and encounter the ground of your own being. Humans come from this ground, as does everything else in nature, and when we get a glimpse of the mystery (or, as the Celts would say, a glimpse beyond the veil), our lives are transformed forever.

This book is written in the spirit of Celtic brotherhood: that is, for all who would come to these pages to learn. You are kin. We hope you will benefit from what we offer here as much as we have. The invisible is real. God bless you all.

CHAPTER 1

Discovering Our Source

The horse and rider are elemental.
They ride at the heart of the wind of God.

— J. Philip Newell

The core concepts in this book were born many years ago while we were traveling in Scotland. We were on our way to the Isle of Mull in the Scottish Hebrides, where we were going to visit the thirteenth-century McCormick castle, the home of our Scottish ancestors. As we ventured toward the town of Oban, we took a detour and got lost in the countryside, which was lush with wild heather adorning the emerald hills. The horizon was ablaze with purple, shrouded by an ephemeral mist. We were awed by the beauty of this rugged highland terrain, and any impatience we had with the detour quickly vanished.

After traveling for many miles, we came upon a wide meadow, where we were forced to stop. The road continued, but we were surrounded by a sea of Scottish sheep, a strange, curious, and adorable lot. They had long shaggy coats and curled horns and were larger than sheep we were familiar with back in the United States. The sheep began sniffing and licking the car and refused to get out of the way. Seeing that it was impossible to move, we finally turned off the engine. We then opened the car doors and prepared to move the animals out of our path, but to our amazement they started flooding into our car. Within moments we had big woolly sheep in every nook and cranny of the vehicle. We thought we might be spending the night literally counting sheep because there was no one in sight to help us move our woolly friends. We took a deep breath and accepted the fact that there was nothing for us to do but succumb to the animals' advances and make friends with them.

Then from out of the mist came the voice of a man with a heavy Scottish brogue. He let out a roar, laughing heartily as he came to the top of the hill and saw our predicament. Hearing his voice, we jumped, since we'd not seen even a sign of another human being for miles.

As this Scottish shepherd approached us, he waved his crook with his gnarled hands and said to the sheep, "You found them!" After this brief exchange with his sheep, he turned to us and said, "My sheep tell me you are on the path. They want to go home with you, but I told them you live a long way from our hillside village. They know you are unusual people."

Our first thought was, What path could he possibly be talking about? All we knew for certain was that we were delayed, tired, and at a dead end.

In his heavy accent, the shepherd asked what we needed. We explained that besides being waylaid by his sheep, we were lost. We had taken a detour and had somehow gotten off the road. He smiled and said, "You're not lost. You've come to the right place. I have been waiting for you. My sheep informed me you were coming. Please stay and have something to eat. I will send you on your way tomorrow."

Intrigued by his hospitality and playful demeanor, we accepted his offer.

That night we were put up as his guests in his tiny village. We conversed with our host long into the wee hours of the night. He told us stories about the Celts in the Hebrides, opening our eyes to a way of life we had never imagined until that moment. After a long and full evening of robust conversation, laughter, and a meal, we collapsed in our beds while the Scottish shepherd continued tending his sheep. In fact, we never caught this wise man taking a wink. He possessed boundless energy and a gentle radiance, though he seemed to be eternally awake, always with one eye open watching his beloved sheep.

To this day we remember him vividly — a kind, wise old man with a twinkle in his eye, who told us stories of Celtic saints and Celtic healings. He assured us that one day we would find ourselves on a spiritual journey and our lives would be very different than they had been up till then.

We didn't take his predictions seriously at the time, for we were busy with our careers and gave little attention to other matters. Eventually, though, that encounter with the shepherd would come to haunt us, his wisdom seeming to follow us like a benevolent presence.

Upon returning to the States, we discovered that we hadn't even known our friend's name. When we spoke of him, we called him "the shepherd."

Years passed, and the encounter fell from our minds, but true to the old man's prophecies, we found ourselves on a spiritual journey, encountering divinity in many forms and guises. We became completely absorbed in the horse business and spent many years using these beautiful creatures in a therapeutic way to help emotionally troubled humans. Messages of a spiritual nature were often communicated to us through our conversations with these ordinary people, but they were particularly strong in our relationships with our horses.

Then one day, while dealing with a tragic injury to one of our horses, we suddenly recalled our encounter with the old shepherd, years before, on the back road in Scotland. Until that day, we had tucked away, somewhere deep in our consciousness, the stories of seemingly magical healings the shepherd had told us.

At dawn we had gone out to feed the horses, as was our habit, and to our horror we saw that Maximo, our beautiful healing horse, had something seriously wrong with his eye. In fact, we couldn't even see the eye, which seemed to have disappeared into his head. Maximo was in obvious pain. We immediately called our veterinarian, who came out to our place, examined the horse, and reported that the eye had been sucked up into the socket. Her most immediate concern was infection. She medicated Maximo and left, planning to return the following morning to perform a follow-up procedure. We were distressed and in pain ourselves. It was then that our memory of the old shepherd came back to us. We recalled his stories of healing along with the vivid details of how those healings were performed.

We called upon God, within and without. We visualized a loving, healing light within us, in our hands and in Maximo. We then tenderly placed our hands over his injured eye and called upon God in all of us to take over. Just as the shepherd had described, what we experienced was a "Thy will be done" sort of ritual. If healing were to occur, it would come from a much higher source than ourselves.

Following our prayer ritual, we ended our day with Maximo and went home. We continued the healing ritual with a meditative prayer that the wise old Scotsman had taught us.

The next morning the vet arrived promptly at 7 A.M. She

examined Maximo, and to her astonishment she found the eye had returned to normal. It was completely healed! We were overjoyed as Maximo gazed back at us with both his healthy eyes; it was as though the old Scotsman was also looking back at us through those eyes, smiling. In time we would discover that not only had Maximo's eye been healed, but something within us had been healed as well.

Following this event, we knew for certain that we had experienced something quite extraordinary. We had encountered a reality beyond our own senses, witnessing firsthand the powers of what we would come to call the *regenerative source* that is rooted in all of life. This experience opened our minds to the tremendous potential available to all of us. Yet it also made us aware that we could not fully know this source unless we lived passionately and were willing to look within. Like so many others in modern life, we had had our doubts about this other reality. But now it was quite clear to us that we needed to trust ourselves to read the signs, to learn to understand the hidden language of the heart. Somehow we knew that it would be only through firsthand encounters that we would begin to *know* the ineffable source of that invisible reality. Now it was time to put what we'd learned into practice.

We became increasingly aware of an important shift in our approach to life. We were no longer *pursuing* spirituality; rather, we were awakened to the divine mystery, the invisible world of meaning and connectedness. Our horses, as our messengers or animal guides, led us along this intriguing path, and over time, we would watch as they guided countless others to experience more expansive realms of consciousness. More and more, we sensed the shamanic influence of the wise old shepherd we'd met in Scotland, whose gentle presence now followed our every step as we met others on the road and shared our experiences.

OTHERS ON THE ROAD

Our psychospiritual journey began with our work as psychotherapists treating severely emotionally disturbed people. Then we brought in our horses as healing partners. While our experiences with patients planted the seeds of our eventual change, our deepening involvement with horses encouraged us to nurture those seeds, and we began to experience a more mysterious side to life.

Through running our equine programs, we began to hear stories about other people's remarkable encounters with horses. People from a wide cross-section of careers and professions reported that they had met spirit horses. They described horses that live between the visible and invisible worlds, traveling back and forth between these worlds according to the needs of the humans in their lives. These interactions with spirit horses could be as subtle as a gentle breeze or as aggressive as a hammer blow. But they were always distinct and unforgettable.

What we began to observe is that the horse instinctively knows how and when to introduce humans to the unexpected and to the challenges of surprises and new difficulties. The horse becomes not only a soothing friend but a provocative adversary — what Celtic shamans call an *anam cara,* or "soul friend," in Gaelic. It is this combination of soothing our doubts and fears and challenging our entrenched behaviors and beliefs that epitomizes the role of the *anam cara.* With laserlike precision, the horse easily assumes the role of soul friend, disturbing our comfort by frustrating our demands, withdrawing its compliance, becoming hard to handle, or shocking our rigid and deterministic minds. Thus, the horse is capable of opening doors of awareness that stretch the bounds of human consciousness.

Over the years we've been privileged to witness this special relationship between horses and their human counterparts many times. For example, there's the story of Laurie, who had been diagnosed with and treated for breast cancer, only to discover another tumor several years later. When the second tumor was found, Laurie was immediately scheduled for emergency surgery. She was terrified, since she did not know what the doctors would find once the surgery began. Laurie and her husband prayed that the tumor would be operable and had not metastasized. However, both were secretly pessimistic. They had heard that when a tumor of this kind returns, it is usually a death sentence. Laurie was only forty-five years old and newly married. Understandably, her husband, Mark, was also terrified, fearing he would lose her.

Mark was a kind and responsible man but had trouble relaxing and enjoying himself. He had a somewhat pessimistic view of life, always waiting for the other shoe to drop. Whenever life went smoothly, he felt a sense of dread, fearing that a catastrophe would surely follow. Having had cancer once, Laurie had been reluctant to marry, but Mark had bravely insisted he could handle whatever came up. Now, as he faced the harsh realities of Laurie's prognosis, he did not feel so valiant. He withdrew emotionally and became increasingly uncommunicative, which was his way of dulling his anguish.

In response to Mark's behavior, Laurie felt abandoned and vulnerable, not only fearing the disease but now growing increasingly anxious that Mark was withdrawing his love. Laurie cried alone, hiding the truth of what she was feeling. It was a disturbing time for both Mark and Laurie, each silently distraught and secretly fearful of what was ahead.

On the day of Laurie's surgery, Mark stayed with her until she dozed off from the anesthesia. Laurie felt frightened as she watched her husband's face fade away. During the operation Laurie felt no pain, but she heard the doctors talking. The tone of their voices and the words they used made her anxious. They sounded so gloomy and foreboding.

Laurie began to panic, but at that moment a beautiful white winged horse appeared in her mind's eye. It radiated light, and it mesmerized her. In that moment all her terror dissolved, and this majestic creature transported her to a magical world, a place that sparkled and was full of love. Laurie felt herself enveloped in a sensation of complete and utter tranquillity. A white light encircled her and the horse. It was as if they were on a different planet.

As she looked around her, she saw many beautiful horses. They had manes and tails of silver and spun gold. They smiled at her, celebrating her presence, and their joy was truly contagious. Some of the horses grazed, while others played or slept. It was so peaceful and inviting. The fields were full of lush green grass, and there was a cool stream that the horses drank from. Wildflowers colored the landscape. Laurie wanted to sing and laugh. She could have rested with them all day, feeling very much at home in this idyllic place.

The white horse that had brought her to this place then motioned for her to follow, and soon Laurie was back in the operating room. The entire episode took only a moment, and then Laurie woke up with a floating sensation. Her entire body felt warm and tingly. As soon as she opened her eyes, she saw her husband's face and felt confident that the surgery had gone well.

Mark informed Laurie that things were very hopeful. The doctors were delighted because the tumor they had found was small, which was not what they had expected. They had removed the tumor, and tests revealed that the cancer had not metastasized.

Some time later, Laurie confided in Mark, telling him she believed that she had been healed by the white horse.

Much relieved by the doctors' optimistic prognosis and by the deeply healing encounter with the white horse, Laurie and Mark shared their fears with each other. Over time they grew much closer and their relationship matured. They both knew they had been given a second chance, and out of the lessons they took away from this experience, they began to trust and confide in each other.

Over ten years passed, and there was no recurrence of the cancer. Then Laurie and her husband went to visit a horse ranch one Sunday afternoon. They loved getting away and spending time in the country. As they walked across an open field, a large white horse approached Laurie. When she looked up, she gasped. The horse stopped directly in front of her. It was the same horse she'd seen in her vision during her surgery over ten years before! Barely able to hold back her tears of joy and gratitude, Laurie looked up into the horse's face and said, "Thank you!" With that, he tossed his head and galloped gleefully away.

To this day, Laurie is certain this was the animal who had carried her away to that healing kingdom. Now, whenever she needs courage in her daily life, she remembers the white horse and his homeland, the invisible land of love.

SACRED BONDS BETWEEN HUMANS AND HORSES

Throughout history, there have been stories about the powerful bonds established between animals, especially horses, and their human counterparts. Those who experience these bonds often cross an etheric threshold where they encounter the sacred nature of their relationship not just with the animal but with their Source. This was the experience of a friend of ours named Michael.

Michael and his gelding, Commandante, were buddies. Michael had bred and raised him along with other Peruvian horses. Commandante was a love, with the kind of disposition people dream of. He would happily comply with anything Michael asked. He was not only a good sport horse but was game for any adventure. As a result, Michael taught him many tricks and complicated reining techniques, which this equine old soul mastered quickly. By the time he was seven, Commandante was a real performer. Michael and his gelding were doing public exhibitions and enjoying every minute of them.

While practicing one day, Commandante lost his balance. Michael assumed that his horse had stumbled on something, and thought nothing of it. However, within a matter of three months, Commandante was tripping and losing his balance more frequently. Then one day Michael saw this very coordinated horse fall down in the pasture for no apparent reason and struggle to get up.

Soon afterward, Michael called a veterinarian to examine him. Commandante was diagnosed with a rare neurological condition that can be caused by a viral infection. The vet informed Michael that there was no known treatment. Michael was devastated. The vet went on to say that it would only be a matter of time before the horse would hurt himself or fall and injure another animal or person. Those words were a death sentence for the magnificent horse.

The veterinarian did not give Commandante much time, so Michael tried to prepare himself for the grievous road ahead. Michael promised the veterinarian that he would put Commandante down before things got too bad.

Over the next six months, Commandante's episodes of instability were fleeting. Michael attributed this, which was atypical of the disease, to the horse's extraordinary ability to control his body. Michael knew Commandante's great heart intimately and knew that he could will himself to stand, even when feeling wobbly. But alas, as time passed the disease worsened, and even with his great heart and will, Commandante could no longer transcend its cruel symptoms. Michael knew the day was approaching when he would have to put Commandante down.

Michael searched for the strength to face the inevitable. Intellectually, he knew there was no choice, but he felt unbearable anguish. It was impossible to imagine life without Commandante. There would be a huge hole left in Michael's heart without his friend. However, it became increasingly clear to him that if the horse was to die in dignity, now was the time.

At daybreak Michael went out to the barn to load Commandante into the trailer and take him to the vet. The horse had ridden in the trailer a hundred times, usually jumping in without any effort. However, on this particular day, he did what Michael dreaded most. Commandante refused to get in.

Separation was going to be hard enough, and now this! Michael had to compose himself to keep from breaking down. As Michael swallowed back his tears, he looked into Commandante's eyes and said, "I could never fool you, old friend! You always knew what was going on. You're right, Commandante, this is not the time for secrets between us. I love you and will miss you. It's your day today."

Michael paused and waited. He was trying his best to read Commandante's signals, but his grief muddled his sensitivity. Michael and Commandante stood quietly, both knowing it was time to let go. Michael decided to see what would happen if he loosened the line and stopped trying to pull and coax the horse into the trailer. When he did, Commandante backed up.

Michael tried to relax and be more attentive to the horse's needs instead of his own. He decided to hold on to the end of the lead line and just follow, to stop trying to control the situation. Michael wanted to find out what Commandante was trying to communicate or where he wanted to go.

The horse headed toward a paddock where Commandante's father lived. As Commandante approached, his father ran to the fence to greet him. Then the two horses breathed rapidly into each other's nostrils and squealed. Following this greeting, they stood together in silence, side by side, almost as if in a state of prayer.

At first Michael thought he was imagining the exchange or projecting his own feelings onto the situation. Yet the longer Michael stood and observed, the more he became convinced that Commandante and his stallion were engaged in an act of devotion. Michael was moved by the tender bond between the two horses. He knew Commandante liked his father, but until this moment he never realized how strong that bond was between them. It seemed that Commandante wanted to pay his last respects. Once this exchange was over, Michael followed Commandante as he stopped and repeated similar exchanges with other horses, saying good-bye to those who had been his friends.

When the horse finished his farewells, he led Michael back to the trailer. Commandante positioned himself in a spot and waited to be loaded. Michael recalls that the horse stood at attention, proudly and stoically signaling Michael that he was ready.

Just before Commandante stepped into the trailer, he paused and turned his head, taking one last look at the place he loved and had always called home. Following this long and intense gaze, he looked directly at Michael, and this time Michael had no trouble reading the signal Commandante communicated: "I am at your command." Commandante marched into the trailer like a proud and noble warrior, obedient and loyal to the very end.

Michael was at Commandante's side as the great horse took his final breaths. The last thing the horse saw before he closed his eyes and slipped into eternal sleep was his beloved Michael. Michael left the veterinarian's feeling very privileged and forever changed.

A month later Commandante appeared to Michael in a vision. He came running to Michael, full of life and spirit. He wanted Michael to know how happy he was because his balance had been restored. To this day Commandante visits Michael in visions from time to time, and Michael can feel his vibrant presence.

Michael now speaks of Commandante as if speaking of a great teacher, one who imparted powerful lessons about tenderness, letting go, and obedience. Commandante showed Michael that to obey can be an ultimate act of love, a sacrifice of the self. He learned from Commandante that to surrender voluntarily is a heroic act, a gift to someone you trust and respect, placing their needs before your own. Michael will never forget Commandante's display of love. In his mind's eye he still sees the horse marching with dignity to his death, obeying Michael's final request.

Michael was so moved by that experience with Commandante that he began to feel a kind of shame over certain aspects of his own behavior. Michael had a history of destroying his relationships by doing the exact opposite of what most people asked. Rebellious and stubborn, he delighted in arbitrarily defying all authority. Many people who came into his life were so offended by his childish behavior that they quickly abandoned him. He pushed everyone away, fearing intimacy.

From time to time Michael would promise himself that he'd turn over a new leaf, but try as he might, he would always return to his alienating behavior. Eventually Michael washed his hands of people and turned to animals as an escape from the volatility of his human relationships.

Through Commandante's noble death, in which the animal

revealed the unbounded strength of his heart, Michael gained a new perspective about his own adolescent behavior, which he now saw as hardly noble and surely not the behavior of a grown man. Several months after the death of the horse, Michael turned away from his chronic habit of defying authority, a character flaw he once flaunted like a badge of honor. He began to learn compassion, respect, and sensitivity. Today Michael is convinced that Commandante left this earth to awaken him, to force him to stop hiding and to rejoin the human community. Michael learned it is one thing to love animals and another to hide behind them.

THE GOLDEN THREAD OF MYSTERY

Over the years, we've received remarkably similar feedback from people — from those who have participated in our equine program, our clients, readers of our first book, *Horse Sense and the Human Heart,* and our fellow horsemen and -women — and we have come to recognize that horses offer something beyond excitement and fun. A vast number of people yearn to be in their company, and others sense there are profound lessons to learn from horses. While some have no idea why they feel this way, others intuitively sense that the mere act of being in the company of a horse will be potent and healing. We've come to believe that being in the presence of horses triggers deep-seated memories, something primal and vital to our human soul.

As we learn to listen, the lessons provided by horses can awaken us to our connection with the Source of our being, bringing us closer to our own spiritual identity. While this connection is never absent from our lives, it can be veiled by the concerns of everyday existence or by the chimera we create within our own minds. The Source whispers rather than shouts. It woos us, most often becoming visible as strands of the finest gold thread woven into the mysterious tapestry of our day-to-day lives. It lingers in all the places we frequent, waiting like a dear friend for our acknowledgment of its presence.

Glimmers of this presence are often embedded in the most mundane and unlikely places, in chance encounters like our meeting with the wise shepherd in the emerald hills of the Scottish highlands. Ultimately, whether in a chance meeting, in literature, on the back of a horse, or in a transcendent connection in nature, we find our way to this creative but hidden world not by entering an otherworldly place but through a journey within. As Carl Jung put it so eloquently, we can understand our lives only "in the light of inner happenings." Out of this illumination of awareness and self-education, we discover what is happening in our own hearts and minds. This is the quest, for if divinity lies within, we can begin to know it only through our own experience and inquiry — by paying attention to what draws or repels us, by tracking our roaming minds to see where they take us, by noticing our own pretenses. It is by monitoring and being alert to our own inner process, to our individual reactions to life situations, to unusual experiences and our unique proclivities, that we begin to see a masterful hand at work in our lives.

Our Scottish shepherd, those many years ago, led us to see that our greatest allies in our quest for greater understanding are often those unexpected encounters that bring us closer to our Source. Some of our greatest lessons have been, and continue to be, learned through the work with our horses. The further we travel on this path, the more we learn that we are not alone in seeking guidance and wisdom in this way. Throughout the millennia, horses have played a prominent role in religion, spiritual development, and the search for inner wisdom. Glimpses into these realms are woven throughout the stories in the pages ahead, revealing how our wise and beautiful equine friends can help us all more fully realize our birthright — the intimate connection with our Source.

CHAPTER 2

The Wisdom of the Iberian Horse Community

For the Iberian horseman, steeped in the lore of Atlantis, these legends are invitations to a mystical inner world where a person becomes both self-directed and a conduit for God....When equestrians reside in Atlantis, even if it is just in the imagination, harmony and friendship with animals become the ideal and the guiding principle for their lives.

For thirty-plus years we taught psychology and psychiatry at universities in Spain. As we became increasingly familiar with the sacred undercurrent of people's daily lives, that country became our spiritual home. During our travels in Spain, we discovered the rich horse-breeding traditions of the region. We soon learned about the Iberian horse community, and it became our prototypical wisdom community, affording us an entry into the ancient, esoteric ways of being with horses. What we learned from these people and their animals would guide us in our psychospiritual work with horses in the years to come.

Early on, we were impressed by the Iberian ideals with regard to the function, temperament, and movement of the horse. Historically, horses and men on the Iberian Peninsula (which includes Spain and Portugal) joined as partners on the battlefield, in bullfights, and in pageants and religious rites during spiritual pilgrimages. These close partnerships between humans and animals, often involving life-and-death struggles, help to explain why the horse's heritage, training, breeding, and care are so intricately linked with the people's beliefs about God and the mysteries of the universe.

Iberians staunchly maintain that the horse is a gift from God, a gift to help humanity see the light and the truth. Their horses fulfill the role of messengers and illuminators, and spending time with a horse is a way for an Iberian to be in the presence of the One. With the help of the horse, people cultivate this mystical union. Instead of seeking thrills, the equestrian aspires to become the embodiment of the light that shines in the darkness.

The Iberians' philosophies concerning the role of horses in their lives struck an inner chord for us. These people articulated something we had felt intuitively but had seldom heard verbalized. We liked what we heard so much that we determined to learn all we could from these people and their horses, to understand more fully why it was that horse and human were able to form such close bonds.

Those bonds no doubt arose out of early man's dependence on the horse, and the horse on humans, so that the fates of both species were most likely intimately intertwined throughout their mutual evolution. Because of climate changes, changing food supplies, and other variable environmental factors, many ancient peoples spent their lives traveling to distant lands in a seminomadic lifestyle. Trying to find locations that would sustain their herds was a top priority. Optimally, they hoped to find grasslands for grazing or the relative comfort of an oasis in desert lands. Cultivation and animal husbandry would eventually evolve out of the necessity of changing life-styles.

History shows that a deep kinship had already formed by the time the horse was domesticated, which occurred in Spain somewhere between 30,000 and 25,000 B.C. We find evidence for this north of Malaga, Spain, where archaeologists have discovered early cave paintings. In a place called the Sierra of the Yeguas (Mares) there are cave drawings of men leading horses by what appears to be a kind of woven halter, suggesting the beginning of the bond between humans and horses that we know today. The Iberian Peninsula is a treasure trove of equine history, where we can still find a crossroads of ancient cultures and modern ways of life.

To understand Iberian equestrian traditions, one must reach beyond what can be revealed in any physical evidence of the past and examine the culture's mythology. Some of the Iberian people's most romantic notions and sacred beliefs about the horse are rooted in the stories of the mythic city of Atlantis. The Spanish people live close to this myth and thoroughly enjoy the fanciful aspects of life. They love to tell stories and embellish their legends, bringing whatever truths these stories reveal into their daily lives. Perhaps due to their own geographic proximity to the purported location of Atlantis and its mysterious prehistory, they have been captivated by Plato's story of this city.

According to myth, Atlantis was a unique civilization where the relationship between humans and animals reached a zenith. This legendary city was purported to be culturally, spiritually, and scientifically advanced beyond anything known even today. Some maintain that this island, so perfect for raising and breeding horses, blew up, perhaps as the result of subterranean activity. Others claim the island was lost following an earthquake, with volcanic activity literally swallowing the island up. Whatever caused Atlantis's demise, those who believe in these legends agree that, one day, a thriving civilization simply vanished beneath the waves. According to folklore, some survivors fled to Spain, Morocco, Libya, and Ireland, where they already had settlements. Some say that these people journeyed as far as the Near East.

Since the writings of Plato, Atlantis has remained an unsolved mystery. Whether it was real or not, the values and imagery expressed in the legends of Atlantis have helped to shape the Iberian consciousness. While archaeological evidence is scant, folk memory and oral tradition keep these beliefs alive. Some stories place Atlantis in the Mediterranean, others in the Atlantic Ocean beyond Morocco, and still others closer to the Americas. But the lack of conclusive data makes the legend no less real in the hearts and minds of the Iberian people.

Even today, breeders of Iberian horses believe that their exceptional abilities with these animals arise from the influence of the lost continent of Atlantis. So enamored are they of this belief that they look for a mark, called the mark of the Cartujano, underneath the forelock of their horses to identify horses believed to be descendants of the legendary Atlantian line. The prized mark is a swirl of hair with an indentation in the center. We first learned about this when we found it on one of our own stallions, Trianero. To Iberian breeders, this mark distinguishes the horse and its special birthright. As legend goes, horses that have it belong to a mythical line dating back to the horses of Neptune, and they are purported to have enchanting qualities. They are progeny of a lost era. Some Iberians go so far as to say that this physical trait links the horse to the fanciful unicorn.

Many Iberians believe that master equestrians from Atlantis exchanged their knowledge with ancient Libyan kings, who came from a race of very tall, fair-skinned, and blue- or gray-eyed people. This same description of the Libyans, or Atlantes, of western Morocco can be found in the writings of Herodotus, Plato, Diodorus, Siculus, and others.[1]

According to legend, the Atlantians and this noble group of Berbers, both men and women, were exceptional equestrians. These horsemen may have either traveled to India or originated there. Some speculate that it was these fair-haired noblemen on horseback who wrote the Vedas, one of the oldest and most sacred Sanskrit spiritual texts.

Though no one can prove or disprove these legends, it is loosely documented that a group of nobles with fair complexions settled in India, riding chestnut horses. No one knows where they came from or where they went. Their origins as well as their fates are shrouded. However, there is record of a spiritually minded group of noble warriors who fit their description and character around 2000 B.C.

Ultimately, if we are to understand the Spanish horse and its role in the lives of the Iberian people, determining the truth of the myth isn't important. Rather, we must understand how this mythology has set the stage for the horse-human interactions that exist in Iberia today.

PLATO'S STORY

In the early stages of civilization, according to Plato, Atlantis was a blessed island where men and women lived close to their divine nature. They lived in harmony with all of God's Creation. During that legendary epoch, humanity was thought to have reached a spiritual apex. All citizens of Atlantis possessed a unique, highly developed state of compassion and respect. Since the men and women of Atlantis had reached such a point, legend goes, there was no end to human creativity and peace. People lived in a land of abundance and prosperity. The animals were happy and well fed, the weather mild, and the fellowship unmatched.

Atlantis was idyllic for equestrians because the island was ruled by the Roman god Neptune (Poseidon to the Greeks), the god of the sea and the patron saint of horses. In mythology Neptune's horses represent the cosmic forces of primordial chaos, which can either destroy people or lead them to their inner powers of divinity.

Since Neptune was the Roman god responsible for creating the horse, it makes sense that the city he ruled would be considered the consummate place for horse breeding. Neptune's horses, like the chestnut horses that would one day be ridden by nobles of India, had golden manes and bronze hooves.

For the Iberian horseman, steeped in the lore of Atlantis, these legends are invitations to a mystical inner world where a person becomes both self-directed and a conduit for God. That world epitomizes a psychic space where the individual can learn to become an original, shaped by infinite challenges and trials. This is the path the Iberian horseman or -woman travels. When equestrians reside in Atlantis, even if it is just in the imagination, harmony and friendship with animals become the ideal and the guiding principle for their lives. With hearts aligned with God, one's intentions become pure and more perfectly attuned to the natural world.

In fact, there are symbolic figures — the cross and circle — that are culturally important to the Iberians, representing a mystical place believed to be on the island of Atlantis where four rivers converged, which symbolizes the restful center of our being. It is the inner sanctuary where we are closest to God. We see similar manifestations of this in the book of Genesis, in stories of Shangri-la and Paradise, and in the stories of Camelot.

It is this state of union, or oneness, symbolized by the cross and circle that the Iberians work to achieve through their relationships with their horses. Yet they are also realistic enough to know that this sense of union or grace does not come easily. Achieving this state requires not only equestrian skills but also a form of what can best be called spiritual cross-training. This spiritual cross-training is an interior process that leads to a new kind of psychological flexibility. The horsemen of old knew that this inner work, geared toward radical transformation, required them to develop an auxiliary set of psychological and spiritual strengths, beyond the normal equestrian skills. It also required that they retain their sense of humor, practicality, and lightness. Humans in quest of the mystical with horses clearly followed a different path than the one followed by the average horsemen and -women of today.

THE HORSEMANSHIP OF IBERIA: LIVING ART ON HORSEBACK

The riding style in Iberia is very unusual. It expresses a progressive philosophy and method of horsemanship, breeding, and training that embody what we are told existed in the legends of Atlantis. The first records of this approach, called the classical method, appeared over twenty-three hundred years ago. Known as the father of the classical method, the Greek cavalry officer and historian Xenophon first wrote on this subject around 400 B.C. This method had been brought to Greece much earlier by an Indo-European invasion that began in 2800 B.C. and lasted until 2000 B.C. As one contemporary history states, "These alien, Indo-European invaders were horsemen, skilled in the handling of their war chariots and apparently invincible. They first conquered, and then over the centuries settled among, the original inhabitants of the Greek peninsula. By 1600 B.C., this union of invaders and natives had evolved into a distinctive culture that spread throughout mainland Greece."[2] Xenophon's treatise on horsemanship provides the fundamentals for all the refined forms of contemporary riding we see today. Offshoots include Latin Dressage, German Dressage, Centered Riding, Hunter-Jumper, and Three Day Eventing; some classical principles are used in the Western tradition as well.

The classical is a natural method that advocates gentleness and harmony between horse and rider in all endeavors. Horse and rider are encouraged to develop such refined and loving communication that they become one. When this classical method is followed, the communication often becomes telepathic. Rider and horse progressively learn to read each other by gaining intimacy and attunement. They appear to be connected by an invisible thread and are sensitive to each other's subtle energy shifts.

The rider rides not only physically but also with his or her mind, spirit, and innermost soul. The horse is encouraged through systematic gymnastic exercises to remain joyful, generous, and happy. Hence, both horse and rider learn to give to each other willingly and lovingly. The horse that performs generously and without reserve can learn to do all the movements that it does in the wild, but at the request of the rider. In the classical method, the horse is engaged by the human to be an active and cognizant participant. The rider strives to cultivate within the horse a wholehearted desire to answer his or her requests with a loud and loving yes.

Witnessing these equestrian traditions in real life made a huge impression on us, and it inspired the work we would later do with our clients. Since the Iberians work their horses in such a superlative way, it was reasonable to assume that they had very advanced ideas about the horse-human interaction. Their degree of intuition, passion, poise, rhythm, and unity is unsurpassed.

Today, there are two modern offshoots of the classical method, the Latin and German schools. The Latin school originated in Spain and Portugal, where it is referred to as Doma

Classica; it is reputed to be one of the finest and most arcane branches of the equestrian arts.

Historically, these two distinct branches of classical riding emerged as a result of working with different breeds of horses. The German school was more concerned with precision and mechanics. The indigenous breeds of horses native to Germany and Iberia had distinct temperaments, ways of moving, talents, and body types. Additionally, how each group used their horses, particularly during wartime and colonial expansion, also shaped their equestrian tradition.

The Latin school developed a method to suit their naturally poised, sensitive, willing, yet hot-blooded Iberian horse. With this temperament, the horse became a natural for a skirmish type of fighting. In the skirmish style, the horse needed to be very swift, nimble, and at times able to go airborne in order to attack and retreat. The horse of Spain was capable of moving at any given time in any of the four directions, just as a dancer uses the box step as a building block for all other dances. Later the horse learned to leap in the air, stand on its hind legs, do an about-face, prance in place, and trot slowly, suspended in air.

Although many of the feats needed for successful skirmish-style fighting may be difficult for less agile horses, the Iberian horses were naturals. Another characteristic ability of the horse was to rise in *masse lavades,* turning about fast and retreating at a gallop, which is called *a volte face.*

The Latin, or Spanish, school is more akin to the classical style that Xenophon describes. The rider shifts his or her weight to help the horse balance and rebalance itself under the saddle. The rider does not rely on physical aids such as hands and legs to drive the horse forward or guide it. Even today, the most highly developed aid must be the mind and heart of the rider instead of the physical body. Stillness of body and mind is stressed. The minds of horse and rider must learn to work together under all circumstances.

Other riding disciplines are found in Spain, of course, but they all echo the traditions found in the classical method — particularly the exquisite merging of horse and rider. Because of the demands to ride with precision, passion, and poise, the rider must temporarily surrender Ego. Disciplined, rigorous, and artistic, with roots in a military tradition where one's skill could make the difference between life and death, the Iberian approach to horsemanship goes far beyond recreation, carrying one into the sacred.

Iberian arts of horsemanship transcend even the bounds of gender, thus cutting through cultural biases and prejudices. We found, for example, that many women in Spain are masters of the Iberian ideals. Some women are even skilled at Rejoneo (Reining), the ancient art of bullfighting on horseback. In modern-day Rejoneo performances in Spain, women wear the same attire as men and must perform the same movements. There are no special concessions for either sex. All must ride with the same discipline and courage. Performing as one, horse and rider are elevated to a spiritual level and any consideration of gender becomes irrelevant and immaterial.

The Lineage of the Iberian Horse:
An Animal Envoy

The Iberian horse, particularly the Portuguese Lusitano of today, is given the esteemed title "Son of the Wind." While this appellation may seem straightforward and literal, to the Iberian people it is more deeply rooted in the generative mystery of life. It also holds the keys to the hermetic process of spiritual transfiguration.

The significance of this legend can be traced back to ancient times when people held different beliefs about conception. For instance, "Virgil, in all seriousness, attributed the fertilizing of the mares to the Zephyr wind (Georgica 1: 273)."[3] Early peoples maintained that the natural elements, such as rain, wind, lightning, and the ocean, were fertilizing agents of the One Source. Within this conceptual context, Son of the Wind confers upon the horse a spiritual or holy paternity.

As in ancient times, horses are part of the modern-day Spanish heart and soul. Many modern breeders treasure their national horse and passionately strive to preserve its history, ancient customs, and legends. The Iberian horse is a living legacy, embodying the ideals of cultural diversity and peace. Tracing its history provides greater insight into the role it has played, and still plays, in people's lives, and why such pride and care go into the breeding of this animal.

Today the Iberian horse is known in Spain as the Andalusian and in Portugal as the Lusitano, but they are essentially the same horse. The Peruvian horse and the Paso Fino are ancient Iberians that arrived on the shores of the New World with the conquistadors, beginning in 1493. Because Peru is isolated, with the ocean on one side and the Andes on the other, the Peruvian horse remained pure. There has been little opportunity for breeding with other horses. In modern times the Iberian and its descendants are referred to as *pura raza español,* meaning "pure Spanish blood."

The three main breeds that contributed to what we now call "pure-blooded Spanish horses" were the Iberian Sorraia, the Moroccan Barb, and the Celtic, or Galician, pony. Spanish horses carry a gene pool with varying degrees of these three breeds. Love and profound reverence for the horse were common threads we have found among the ancient Iberian, Moroccan, and Celtic cultures. Each added a richness and sanctity to the process of animal husbandry. As one delves deeply into the lineage of the Iberian horse, one finds cultures that perceived God's face peering back at one through the eyes of the horse.

The Horse Breeding of the Carthusian Monks

Southern Spain is one of the most famous horse-breeding regions of the world. The area from Seville to Jerez de la Frontera is renowned for its breeding farms. In addition to the area's private breeding farms, monks also bred horses, concentrating their efforts on one of the finest lines of Andalusian horses. This order of Carthusian monks (Catholic contemplatives) began pursing their passion for horse breeding when Don Alvaro Obertus de Valeto gave the fathers of Cartuja a sizable piece of ranchland in 1476. They continued this horse-breeding endeavor until approximately 1835. The monks not only significantly contributed to breeding Andalusian horses but also preserved a coveted bloodline within the breed called the Cartujano, which has a strong resemblance to the Baroque horse. The Cartujano was bred for its concentration of genes from the early Barb, which came to the Iberian Peninsula before the birth of Christ.

Achieving harmony with all of creation was one of the main goals of these monks. They not only bred magnificent horses, but they lived, learned, and prayed with their animals. One thing that makes this breed so sensitive to humans is that their specific job for centuries has been tending to the human soul — truly taking the role of the *anam cara,* or soul friend. On the walls of a Carthusian monk's stable, an inscription about the horses reads, "Leap into Heaven."

The Moroccan Barb

Morocco, a neighbor to southern Spain, played a preeminent role in the history of the Iberian horse, with her native Barb being a key contributor to the Spanish horse's gene pool. The Barb, a very graceful, athletic, tractable, and energetic horse, evolved from an ancient breed found originally in Libya and Persia.

We know the Moors brought philosophy, mysticism, and art to Spain, but they also brought their horse expertise. The Muslim love of the horse is repeatedly mentioned in the Koran: "When God created the horse He said to the magnificent creature: I have made thee as no other. All the treasures of the earth shall lie between thy eyes. Thou shalt cast thy enemies between thy hooves, but thou shalt carry my friends upon thy back. Thy saddle shall be the seat of prayers to me. And thou fly without any sword. Oh, horse."4

The Portuguese Sorraia

Portugal, at one time part of Spain, is only a stone's throw from Andalusia. The Portuguese horse, called the Sorraia, is another ancestor that has played a significant role in the development of the Iberian. This horse is native to an area in Portugal where two rivers, the Sor and the Ria, converge. In this area, wild horses and bulls lived together. The bull was one of the horse's natural enemies.

Since the Sorraia shared a habitat in Portugal with wild bulls, it developed a keen sense for the behavior of its bovine counterpart. One thing it learned was that running from bulls didn't work. Hence, the Sorraia developed agility and wit. These horses are expert at outsmarting and pivoting away from bulls. Due to this innate understanding of wild bulls, the gene pool of the Sorraia was a natural for developing a horse capable of bullfighting from horseback.

As the Portuguese relied more and more on their horses for the bullfight, the ritual fight eventually became a religious ceremony. Even today the Portuguese use their horses for this sacred purpose. Horse and rider must unite to conquer the dark side, symbolized by the bull. This metaphor is similar to that of the modern bullfight, which enacts the struggle between light and dark, life and death, but in this case it is manifest in real-life action and breeding.

The cattle tradition, called Doma Vaquera, is still prevalent in many Hispanic countries today, and here, too, the traits of the Sorraia serve well. This ancient school of horsemanship is the forerunner of the American cowboy tradition. In preparing the horse for this venture, riders often execute reining patterns to prepare the horse. Sometimes these patterns can resemble a labyrinth, or *caricole*, intended to encourage a meeting of the mind and heart.

As an interesting aside, Sorraias were present on Columbus's second voyage to the New World. How they got aboard ship was rather scandalous. Prior to departure, some of Columbus's men used the more expensive Andalusians, which Queen Isabella had intended to send to the New World, to pay off a gambling debt. In place of these royal horses, the crew substituted the modest Sorraias.

The queen was furious. She made sure, on the next scheduled voyage, that some of her finest blood stock from the Royal Stud Farm was aboard. She wanted special bloodlines to be used as foundation stock for the New World. Nonetheless, the Sorraias that had already arrived did very well in the New World because they were hearty, sweet, and very functional.

The Sorraia at the present time is almost extinct, though some people are trying to rescue it from oblivion. We had the pleasure of seeing some of these animals in Mexico. Some are lavender in color and have dorsal stripes. They are very primitive looking, with some stripes on their legs.

The Celtic or Galician Pony

The third horse contributing to the Iberian stock was variously called the Garron, Galician, or Asturian pony. This pony is indigenous to the areas in northwest Spain called Galicia and Asturia, and is also found in Ireland and Scotland. The cultural links among these areas help us to better understand what at first might seem unlikely. For instance, the people known as the Galicians live in an area of northern Spain referred to as Celt-Iberia and consider themselves to be both Spanish and Celtic. The melding of these two cultures is reflected in many ways; for example, the people of this region speak both Spanish and Gaelic, wear kilts, and play Celtic bagpipes.

Interestingly, there is also a strong troubadour tradition in this area, influenced by Sufi mystics from Spain, Persia, North Africa, and Afghanistan, such as Ibn Al' Arabi, El-Ghazali, and Jalaludin Rumi, who wandered and sang about love, longing, and union with God, their beloved. This troubadour tradition from the Middle East and Persia resurfaced in western Europe during the Middle Ages in Celtic Iberia. Their quest and longing for God were the basis for the chivalric (knighted horsemen) traditions so popular in this unique region.

We learn from these cultures that chivalry was originally a mystical tradition in which men worked with horses for a higher good and order. This particularly interested us since our work with horses often required our clients to focus on a higher good, something that would require them to abandon excessive Ego gratification, thus minimizing self-involvement. The knights' quest was to attain a point where all was reconciled and a new creation emerged. At this point, they believed, the false self was crucified and the real (divine) self was resurrected. The chivalrous knight, a mounted warrior and adventurer, shared his life with horses, knowing that this relationship would furnish him with the trials necessary to get closer to that spiritual goal. Horses helped the knight to refine his soul, purify his heart, and elevate his character.

Chivalry comes from the French word *chevalier,* meaning

horseman. It also connotes a gentleman who is courteous, cultured, refined, noble, bold, adventurous, and courageous — someone who has worked to develop his noble or spiritual attributes. As in most spiritual disciplines, the initiates took vows and submitted themselves to the direction of a spiritual advisor. Yet in the case of the knights, the advisor was a horse. In Spain, this kind of gentleman horseman is called a *caballero.* Chivalry was not intended to be something one *did,* but rather was a way of life aimed at developing the person's highest and noblest capacities.

Along with all its cultural richness, Galicia, home of the Galician pony, is a holy site. It is here that we find Santiago de Compostela, or the Cathedral of St. James. St. James, the patron saint of Spain and brother of Jesus, was purported to have mysterious abilities. He is portrayed as coming out of the sea riding a white horse, with his garments covered in cockleshells.

The fact that St. James is riding a white horse is not without significance. The horse has been considered a godsend to the Celts and Iberians, in both pagan and Christian times. The Galician pony, native to this area, is esteemed for its loving, obedient, and faithful temperament, not to mention its ambling gait. Pilgrims during the Middle Ages often rode these palfreys to help them make their sacred journeys.

Hence, this pony has been a central part of Celtic and Iberian social, cultural, and religious life. We find its presence deeply embedded in regional folklore and literature. It is the "palfrey" we read about in Chaucer's *Canterbury Tales* and the legendary mount for the knights of King Arthur's court.

TRADITIONS OF THE SOUL, LOST AND RECLAIMED

Indo-European history and traditions make clear that the relationship between humans and horses was once honored in ways that have become clouded by contemporary life. These traditions demonstrate that working and living with horses, within a spiritual framework, puts one in touch with inner truths and balance that contribute to the evolution of the human psyche. Still today, the special spiritual and emotional bonds between horses and humans are cultivated in Iberian horse communities, which contain wisdom traditions tens of thousands of years old. Whether horses are a part of our everyday lives or not, there is much to be learned about ourselves and our relationship to the Cosmos by exploring the timeless lessons they still offer us.

CHAPTER 3

Animals Awakening the Human Soul

We are never completely free of our egos, but we can work to cultivate a
psyche that recognizes when Ego is getting in our way. We discover again
and again in working with horses that as we gain inner balance, we are
better able to surrender our Egos without collapsing emotionally.

In his book *The Essential Mystics,* Andrew Harvey cites Plato's
analogy of the charioteer as the soul. Harvey points out that
Plato used this image to describe the inner struggle of the spiritual path, and what happens within us when we catch a
glimpse of the Divine Mystery. Harvey writes:

> Each soul is divided into three parts, two being like steeds and
> the third like a charioteer. Now of the steeds, so we declare,
> one is good and the other is not, but we have not described
> the excellence of the one nor the badness of the other, and
> that is what must now be done. He that is on the more hon-
> orable side is upright and clean-limbed, carrying his neck
> high, with something of a hooked nose; in color he is white,

with black eyes; a lover of glory, but with temperance and modesty; one that consorts with genuine renown, and needs no whip, being driven by the word of command alone. The other is crooked of frame, a massive jumble of a creature, with thick short neck, snub nose, black skin, and gray eyes; hot-blooded, consorting with wantonness and vain glory; shaggy of ear, deaf, and hard to control with whip and goad.[1]

The mystical path is one of learning to train our two inner horses, particularly the one that disobeys and puts us in danger. As we have seen so often, riding and working with horses helps us handle this private inner struggle; in our relationships with horses we externalize the inner conflict and begin working with our symbolic charioteer and his two horses in a tangible way. By confronting our inner horses in the real world, we learn to take charge of ourselves under a great variety of circumstances. We develop an appreciation for the importance of inner control, which is so essential for soul realization.

A person working with a horse learns to gain composure in some very heated situations, and with experience learns how to encourage an unruly horse to go where it is guided. A rider who can do this humanely teaches the horse to contain its impulses, resulting in the horse becoming open, willing, and attentive. These experiences with horses can teach us the same lessons we want them to learn: to recognize, contend with, and unify the two sides of our inner nature (the human and the Divine) so that we can ultimately work for a higher purpose.

This work of the soul is tricky, but we persevere in it because it holds the deepest possibilities for lasting joy and more fully realizing our individual potential. It leads to an attention of the heart by progressively gathering and accumulating inner wisdom rather than mere techniques. As the soul grows in its capacity to patiently understand, we gain increasing presence, openness, and attunement.

Over time, we start to experience a new entity emerging from within us, one that is able to receive whatever comes our way. As Jacob Needleman, a modern-day philosopher and religious scholar, writes in *Lost Christianity*, "The point seems to be that something has to be awakened in man that is both highly individual yet at the same time free from mere subjectivity, something both intensely my own yet free of ego. It is referred to, in ancient language, as *that which is between God and the animal*. It is *the intermediate*. Other traditional descriptions speak of a need for something to be *formed* in man; or *collected* (as *"light"* is collected); or *purified*."[2]

This kind of spiritual work isn't glamorous or showy. It holds little appeal for those who want to feel special or who wish to achieve some sort of celebrity. Rather, we advance by actively and incrementally learning to collect our own desires and aims, just as master equestrians have done for centuries with the horse. In this way we learn to live vibrantly and responsibly in this world, even as we cultivate a soaring consciousness. As Andrew Harvey tells us, the soul helps us recognize that there is much more to us and our lives than we can ever imagine.

The World of the Soul

We use the word *soul* in everyday speech — *soul searching, poor soul, dear soul,* and even *soul mate*. More recently, the term *soul friend* has crept into our vocabulary. It comes from the Gaelic *anam cara*, popularized by author John O'Donohue in his book by the same title. O'Donohue describes the *anam cara* as a person with whom we can share all the secrets of our lives. Such a friendship cuts across all conventions, allowing us to be fully recognized and accepted. This person, or animal, is literally a friend of our soul, joining us in ways that transcend our everyday perceptions. This concept of a soul friend is particularly important as we seek to understand what horses have to teach us, how they teach, and why. It helps us to imagine why, for thousands of years, these noble animals have been such an important part of human evolution.

While the word *soul* is familiar, its meaning remains elusive. If we go back five thousand years, we find the Egyptian concept of Ka. According to this carefully articulated theory, a portion of us has an existence separate from the physical body and so survives the death of that body. A few thousand years later, around 384–322 B.C., Aristotle explored a similar concept. He called the portion of us that remains eternal the soul, or *psyche,* the Greek word for soul. Aristotle said the soul nourishes, sensitizes, and furnishes humanity with the capacity for reason and understanding. He believed that without developing our souls, we are incapable of quality living, feeling, and understanding. The soul, he said, is what makes us fully human, reminding us of our origins and our connection to the Infinite.

The Greeks believed the soul or psyche was not limited by time and space, nor was it only rational or irrational. Instead, it was attuned to both sense and nonsense, and possessed no boundaries between the conscious and the unconscious. It took its direction only from a higher power, beyond social conventions and the dictates of merely human influences and pressures. It is little known that Freud worked with the soul because he used the Greek word *psyche.*

Spiritual traditions since the beginning of time have taught that it is through the eternal nature of our souls that we develop the capacity to tolerate, endure, and even peacefully accept conflict, contradictions, incompatibilities, and dualities. As our spiritual perceptions mature in these ways, we open ourselves to a reality beyond polarities and dualities, to an underlying unity. Within that unity our souls expand. We open up to a greater tolerance for dissonance and an acceptance of contradiction. We do so not through martyrdom or masochism, but by living peacefully with that which we cannot resolve. Learning to live intimately with life's contradictions helps us gather energy, wherein, ironically, our creativity swells.

Jacob Needleman tells us that the soul is not a static entity but a movement of energy. As such, the soul allows us to more openly see the world around us, in particular its contradictions, and it even helps us embrace the emotional pain that often surrounds these contradictions. This ever-moving energy of the soul nurtures us toward wholeness until we at last learn to see and accept incongruity in the world, ourselves, and other creatures. From this ability we gain inner harmony even in the midst of inner and outer chaos. We drop illusion and fantasy and, like an eagle, begin to see the bigger picture with exceptional clarity.

In time, seeing what is real, even when it is upsetting, will not shake our inner core. We observe what is — beauty or darkness — without turmoil. As we view our lives from the vantage point of the soul, we learn patience with ourselves and others, and from this acquire the inner strength to abide psychological pain. In working with an unruly horse, we have an opportunity to see this process in action. It is at the point when we can fully accept what is that we are able to respond with patience and proceed in an effective way, one that benefits the horse as well as ourselves. "Whenever there is pain or contradiction," Needleman explains, "this energy of the soul is released or *activated*."[3]

Needleman echoes a theme that Christ taught: *You must die before you live.* As we release ourselves, even momentarily, from the self-importance of the Ego, we are born to a greater truth and purpose. In his book *Christ the Yogi,* Ravi Ravindra, a Hindu philosopher and physicist, reflects on the Gospel of

John from the New Testament. Ravindra contends that the soul strives for the intelligence, fire, and order that are eternal and beyond time, and that cannot be destroyed: "In a certain sense, there is a constant struggle in the soul of every creature between the tendencies of light and those of darkness, between that which comes from Above and that which pulls one down. In the midst of this struggle, each one can be assured by the scripture that the eternal Light continues to shine, summoning us to be rightly ordered and to dwell in the wisdom of the True Word."4

The inward journey requires us to radically shift our perceptions and attitudes — to stop thinking things must go our way or as planned, and to acknowledge imperfections in ourselves and others without rage, hatred, prejudice, or intolerance. Following this path, we uproot our assumptions and preconceived ideas. We become exposed and able to love. Horses can play a role in this evolution, as the personal stories in this book make clear.

As we continue to travel on the inward journey, we develop intuitive radar. The mystic Julian of Norwich speaks of this new sense when she tells us we can gain an ability to know *all is well* even in the midst of tragedy, for then we truly begin to identify ourselves with a greater reality. Aristotle tells us that our experience extends far beyond our normal sensory perceptions and mental processes. We discover and cultivate a different kind of mind and heart, one that *accesses* truth rather than *invents* it. Drawing from Plato's metaphor of holding the reins of two horses, one wanton and hard to control, the other guided from within by honor and temperance, it is the latter that now carries us forth.

Once activated, the mystical mind and heart hunger to resume a relationship that has been interrupted — the torrid and timeless love affair between God and the soul. While we have all known this relationship before, our memory of it, in most cases, is suppressed soon after birth.

In many cultures the soul is symbolized by the dove because of the dove's fertile and life-giving properties. It gives wings to the human personality. It is the feminine Sophia, bearer of wisdom, which is represented in Christian nomenclature as the Holy Spirit. The Song of Songs in the Old Testament gives us insight into the romantic and pensive nature of the soul. The soul and God are always portrayed as two lovers, aching to unite upon realizing they have been separated. They live to embrace and reflect each other's light.

Our first priority is to progress through normal phases of human development and attend to worldly affairs. However, once these building blocks are laid, this buried memory of the soul may slowly return to consciousness, resulting in an urge to rest and commune with the Divine Presence.

Our soul, unlike our other human faculties, flowers by a process of lingering. It has a different learning style than the human intellect. It absorbs lessons in indirect ways — by exposure, immersion, and osmosis. We learn as if by transfusion. In this state of union with the whole, knowledge and strength flow from one being into the other.

Paradoxically, even though our souls are nourished by resting in the Divine Presence, we do not become lazy or inattentive to the people and activities around us. Instead we enjoy our interactions and participate even more than before. We learn that resting is not dropping out. It is slowing down, acquiring wisdom by savoring experience.

Our attention heightens and improves because we are alert to any signs of the Beloved. We notice the little things around us: trivia, nuances, glances, aromas, hints of beauty. We become detectives of love. We move from being satisfied with gross observation to a more subtle and refined kind of attention. "As we shall see, the world of attention is the world of the human soul," says Needleman.[5] We have all experienced this when we are in love.

Working with horses in a therapeutic setting, we are presented with the immediacy of establishing a relationship in which lack of alertness gets immediate feedback in the form of unruly, indifferent, confused, or rebellious behavior from the animal. Our attentiveness gains us love. By living through our life lessons and refining our attention, we encourage our soul to take wings. As Christopher Bamford writes in his reflections on the ninth-century Irish theologian John Eriugena, "Naturally simple, the soul passes through different states and is called by different names; mind, spirit, or intellect, when it contemplates divinity; reason, when it considers created things; sense, when it perceives and acts in the world of the senses; life, when it endows with life. As Eriugena stresses, the intellect is not the maker but the discoverer of natural arts, but it finds them within, not outside itself."[6]

We come into this world with a biological and psychological need to survive. As a result, we initially adhere to a simple rule: *first things first.* As we focus our attention on the maintenance of our physical beings, our memories of soul and God fade. This healthy and necessary amnesia continues until we can learn to love without losing our minds and shirking worldly responsibilities. Meanwhile, our survival — both physical and psychological — becomes dependent upon that portion of our beings that we call ego. Through our submission to the ego, we not only lose sight of our relationship with God but develop a whole new set of perceptions dedicated to our welfare in the physical world.

WHERE EGO REIGNS

Without being tempered by the soul, the ego becomes the Ego, with a capital *E,* and keeps us earthbound. This is because the ego's prime goal is defense and acquisition, not love, expansiveness, or sacrifice. When love is Ego-motivated, we typically find we have ulterior motives, though they may be subconscious or unconscious. For example, a person might seek love in order to feel whole and complete.

The ego is just an aspect of the psyche, one that we need for decision making, neutralizing our strong emotions, making judgments, and coping with hard times. It can help us filter and discriminate when there is too much information or stimulation. It can help us integrate complex experiences and even assist in the formation of new relationships. But we also need to be aware that the more we indulge it, the more we become like spoiled, self-serving children. This regression occurs because the ego also helps regulate our sense of self; when we are stroked too much or undeservedly, we lose a balanced sense of who we are. A false sense of self evolves and soon dominates. In our work and in this book, we like to call this distorted ego "the Ego" when it takes on a separate identity and serves the material brain. It is the Trickster. It fools us into believing we're doing great, even when we're not. It starts to think for us.

The ego that Freud described was of the mind. A healthy ego does not think; it just is. It serves the psyche and works in concert with the superego and the instincts. It does not try to rule the psyche but rather works in harmony with it. By contrast, the Ego always wants more. It demands power until it becomes a controlling and destructive force. This entity develops its own false self that convinces us it is real. It is a parasite, growing like a cancer cell that ultimately annihilates its host.

Like Plato's unruly steed, consorting with wantonness, our egos can easily get out of control and become Egos. For example, think about what has happened in modern society, with so much emphasis placed on the self, often under the guise of ego-centered self-esteem. Those who are products of what some have called the self-cult not only fail to achieve real self-esteem but end up with little or no respect for themselves or anyone else. True relationship becomes increasingly challenging, and true union with another impossible. We've learned from this that when we put too much emphasis on the self, dissociating ourselves from others, we tend to become preoccupied with getting more and more *goodies* in the temporal world. Lacking enduring values and focused on acquisition, we become insatiable. When overfed, Ego becomes greedy. Envy builds, with pervasive feelings of emptiness. We lose our creative edge and potential. In horse jargon, we kill our spirit.

Most of us are seduced by our own Egos to one degree or another. We like to think of our goals as selfless, for example, when in fact they bring us considerable pleasure. For example, we "sacrifice" twelve hours of our free time each week to do community work. While that work benefits others in many ways, it also brings us pleasure to know that we are making a positive difference. Not that there is anything wrong with seeking self-benefit, unless it is extreme; it is part and parcel of our human nature.

We are never completely free of our egos, but we can work to cultivate a psyche that recognizes when Ego is getting in our way. We discover again and again in working with horses that as we gain inner balance, we are better able to surrender our Egos without collapsing emotionally. A healthy ego is necessary for spiritual maturity, though there comes a time when we choose to put aside all self-interest in pursuit of a higher goal. The best way to guard against Ego's domination is to be honest and aware of our motives and to increasingly recognize those early clues that our Ego wants to take center stage, relegating God to the shadows.

Though it guides us to become ever mindful, spiritual

development does not require us to do anything rash, such as giving away all our material possessions or stopping dancing or drinking. But we do need to become diligent to make sure that these do not feed our Egos or cloud our awareness of the Ultimate reality. Our goal is to subsume our small "I" under the only "I," which is God, and to understand how to live within the cosmic hierarchy.

Much of spiritual development is about learning what's truly good for "me." It is about learning that self-serving or Ego-motivated thoughts and actions do not always serve the soul. Humans suffer much when they put their own image before God, or they honor an image of God that they themselves have created.

Horses Stirring the Soul

The idea that horses could touch and animate the human soul became a compelling realization for us. Perhaps here was a way to awaken the human soul through nature's guidance. At the time that we came to this realization, such approaches were rare in the self-improvement and spiritual development movements. Except for pet therapy to help the elderly, the mentally ill, or others at risk, animals were rarely consulted, though certainly we knew that they could enrich the human experience and guide our souls.

At the same time, we knew the repercussions of psychotherapies that failed to acknowledge and work with the human soul. People turning to these therapies for help often came away feeling confused, bitter, or cheated. Often they stayed stuck in old habits of obsessing about their woes. Or, as Stanislav Grof points out in his book *Spiritual Emergency,* "Some of the dramatic experiences and unusual states of mind that traditional psychiatry diagnoses and treats as mental diseases are actually crises of personal transformation, or 'spiritual emergencies.'"[7]

During this period when we were observing the limits of psychotherapies that ignored the soul, we were witnessing the healing power of nature on the soul. There seemed to be nothing quite as healthy, sobering, and humbling to the human Ego as a confrontation with nature, which forced a healthy shift in the balance of power away from the Ego. Our own personal experiences with horses had convinced us not only that this was so but that others could benefit by this kind of personal encounter with the natural world.

It has been a great awakening to witness what happens to people in a natural setting, such as when they learn to seek equine wisdom for enlightenment and spiritual growth. In this radical shift in the hierarchy, animals take the lead and humans follow, which is exactly what the human species needs. In our age of high-tech, high-stress living, the soul in this way expands with the heart of nature. Indeed, it became clear to us that this connection with nature, through our connection with horses, was the missing ingredient to help humanity's spirit soar. As one man aptly stated to his wife, "Since you have been riding horses, you are like a fish who has found water."

For many, this renewal, through the guidance of horses, opens inner doors and reveals divine intelligence. The revelations experienced in the natural world typically spark an interest in the sacred and lead us all to an even deeper spiritual search.

THE GIFT OF FORESIGHT:
ESCORTING US BACK HOME

This is exactly what happened with us, for it was one of our own mares who led us down this more spiritual path. We had been happily immersed in the equine therapy business, and our attitudes about healing had significantly changed. Living with horses so closely had created new patterns in our hearts.

As a result, we found ourselves in some unusual circumstances. We began to get a reputation in the equine world as people who understood dangerous horses. One day, some of our friends asked us to rescue a mare, Alicia, from abuse (a story that we also describe in our first book, *Horse Sense and the Human Heart*). This event provided us with another opportunity to see a miracle emerge from chaos and tragedy. What we didn't know was that Alicia, our golden mare, was escorting us back home. Our soul's journey with God had begun.

When we rescued Alicia, she was aggressive. Even when she was out of immediate danger, she acted disturbed. She would jump back and forth from her hind legs to her front legs and then kick out aggressively, her ears pinned, a sure sign that she was very agitated. She was fighting an invisible enemy. Many of her gestures reminded us of the human patients we worked with in psychiatric hospitals.

It was obvious that Alicia was in her own world. She would periodically lunge toward us aggressively, showing her teeth as a reminder for us to keep our distance. We respected her warnings and gave her plenty of space when she needed it. During that time, we resorted to whispering. We took turns sitting in her stall quietly and whispering when appropriate. Adele spearheaded the mission, since it is easier for a horse to bond with one person at a time, most particularly when the horse is mad.

Adele spent hours every day in Alicia's open pipe stall. When Adele got tired, we relieved her. While sitting in Alicia's stall, we prayed, whispered, meditated, and daydreamed. We felt helpless because it seemed that we were making no progress with her. For weeks, we had no visible signs that what we were doing was working. Nonetheless, we blindly stuck with it, making no judgments and projecting no expectations about the future.

About six weeks passed, and then we got the first indications that our efforts were paying off. Alicia made a sudden and unexpected breakthrough. She started approaching and sniffing us. From that point forward, we quickly gained her trust. The turnaround she made was phenomenal. The degree of trust she recovered, after being so emotionally wounded by human beings, was a miracle.

Yet something about being together and prevailing in our efforts had created an unusual bond between us. Adele and Alicia had cultivated an exceptionally close relationship. Even after Alicia's breakthrough, Adele had a strong desire to continue her practice of sitting with her, though she had no idea why she was doing this or where she was going with what had become an activity that no longer seemed necessary or perhaps even useful. As Adele acted upon her strange urges to do nothing but repose with Alicia, she began to get *impressions* from the horse. What she received was not words but images and directives. Initially, Adele felt a sense of frustration as she tried to understand what Alicia was trying to communicate. Then one day a message came through in the form of a clear mental image.

It happened as we were beginning to change some of our theories and instructional methods in our therapy work. We were getting more deeply involved in teaching many of our clients about unity on horseback. We guided them to become centaurs (part human, part horse) instead of technicians or passengers. We encouraged them to *commune* with their horses. Then Alicia transmitted this impression: "If you really want to know about communion with horses, go back to church. Learn more about *communion!*" Adele recalls Alicia's deep sense of exasperation with human beings in general.

We had never expected a horse to be telling us to return to church, much less to learn about communion. So when Adele told us what had happened, we were bewildered. We didn't question what had occurred. We had been around horses long enough to know that extraordinary things happen. We had also learned to not take communiqués such as this lightly, for we had had quite a successful track record by paying attention to them. For years they had been right on target with most people who received them from the horses. What perplexed us was the content of this particular message. Why church? Why communion? In truth, going to church was the last thing we wanted to do. We were perplexed and very curious. What did Alicia see that we didn't? Who was training whom? For sure, we were no longer leading. Alicia urged us to follow and trust her wisdom. But sensing she was trying to say something important to us didn't make her message easier to accept, or her "prescription" more palatable.

The whole message seemed incongruent and out of context. It was very humbling. We questioned ourselves: Was there something we had missed? That, in fact, was the case. Alicia furnished the clue that would lead us deep into uncharted territory. Soon we would learn that she and the other horses were pointing us toward a higher level of awareness, one that had become all but lost in the distractions of modern life.

CHAPTER 4

Mysticism and Horses —
An Ancient Way of Being

As we learn to interact with the imago Dei, *or divine presence, in the horse, we do not worship that animal as a god, but we consciously begin to look for and recognize divine attributes residing within it. Through that process the horse sparks an inner expedition, connecting us with the same divine attributes within ourselves.*

In retrospect, it's clear that our perceptions about horses began to change quite radically well before we met Alicia, back when we acquired Trianero, a stallion from Peru. For some time we had had Peruvian horses in our stable, which we had found to be excellent for the therapy work with our clients. But Trianero, our first stallion, stood out from the rest. The story of how he came to us is, in itself, extraordinary, and we tell it in detail in chapter 9. For now, suffice it to say that from his first appearance in our lives his extraordinary charisma and quality of spirit awed as well as puzzled us.

As he walked off the trailer the day he was delivered, he

seemed to us dauntless and unapproachable. But it was his elegant style and commanding presence that struck us most. Once on firm ground, he stood and surveyed his audience, observing us intently as if to make certain we were watching. Suddenly his eyes flashed, and he peered down at our little group, almost daring us to look away. He obviously wanted our full attention, and in that magical moment he got it.

Once certain that we were watching, he began what could only be described as a dance — his way of expressing to us who he was. He captivated us with spectacular movements, such as leaps in midair. Every movement was executed with great deliberation and consciousness. He was exuberant and spontaneous but in no way rebellious or disobedient. More than anything else, it was a statement, and one that made an impact on us that would guide us toward the next level of understanding of and appreciation for the tradition from which he'd come.

Totally captivated by his performance, we drew closer to him. The atmosphere was electric. Trianero had taken us to a place of enchantment. Everyone fell completely silent and remained focused on this extraordinary exhibition of his capacities. Through his dramatic display, we felt small and insignificant. Trianero exuded something special, something ancient and not of this world.

Observing his power and energy on that first day, we assumed we would be unable to handle him. One week later, much to our surprise, we were riding him in the moonlight with neither saddle nor bridle.

It was through Trianero that we began to comprehend what the Spanish mean when they say the Iberian horse has a "noble disposition." From that day forward, this stallion has continued to inspire and teach us about the transcendent spirit.

With Trianero's entrance into our lives, we began to look

at horses differently. He validated what we had felt for many years — that horses embody the sacred and bind us to the life force. Yet this life force, like Trianero himself, is not always comfortable. It has highly charged polarities, generated by paradox, that often throw us into a state of tension and chaos. Unlike the dualism of the human mind that separates the world into this-or-that, either-or, horses teach that both ways are true. Through our acceptance of this paradox of our own perceptions — an insight the horses teach us so well — we begin to see the underlying unity of all things. We are freed from our inner rigidity because the paradox crashes through the illusion of opposites that we so easily create for ourselves.

This, the divinity of paradox, provides us with a tangible way to make contact with the ineffable Source of our being. By stretching our minds, often to the point of absurdity, we open the floodgates to a wellspring of divine attributes within the universe, as well as within ourselves — generosity, love, truth, gentleness, spirit, boldness, loyalty, and graciousness.

Marcia, a woman who recently took one of our equine retreats, wrote about the penetrating nature of the horses and how they helped her find her own divine attributes. These are her words:

> For the past week I have been staying at Three Eagles Ranch in the beautiful Hill Country northeast of San Antonio. The weather here has been as variable as the horses. The rain, wind, and bone-chilling cold at the beginning of the week have given way to milder temperatures with blue skies and gentle breezes. It feels as though nature has echoed my own transformation.
>
> I arrived stiff and apprehensive under the cloud of a migraine. But by midweek, I had begun to soften and open to the beauty surrounding me. One cannot remain impassive and closed off in the presence of the proud and fiery Peruvian Paso horses.

The stallion, Morocco, is stunning to the eye, and his regal bearing makes me want to hold my head up and walk taller through the world. He is the one who says, "Why not change into fire?"

The mares, Mary Magdalena and Alicia, share the stallion's proud heritage but feel gentler to the touch. Magdalena, the redhead, is always the first to come to me at the fence. Alicia, the blonde, is the lead mare and the new mother of Malack, a teddy bear of a colt sired by Morocco.

Surprisingly, Malack does not stay with his mother but instead is tended by Maximo, a gelding who shares my sluggish melancholy. Like me, he is easily defeated. But also like me, he has the potential to come alive. Working with him has been a challenge, but it has made me realize that if Max can lift his head and walk with spirit, so can I. And vice versa. I can give him my energy. I can make a difference. I can be happy, and so can he. Come Max, come Marcia. Come and see.

I can also see something of myself in the black beauty of Alicia's herd, Monserrat Caballe. She is a timid filly, but with guidance and a firm hand she can overcome her fears and move with confidence and grace. Watching Deborah work with her gives me hope for myself.

Although I have had little contact with the elder but grand stallion, Trianero, I can still feel the noble spirit that resides in his frail body. [Trianero is now twenty-nine years old.] He instills in me a desire to persevere, to not give up, to continue the path I make simply by walking on.

All of these animals are beautiful to the eye and soft to the touch, but it is really their spirits that shine through and open my heart. My hope is to carry that spirit with me, to nourish the flame within, as I continue on my journey through life. Why not come and see? Why not, indeed, change into fire?[1]

A prayer emerged for Marcia from her week's experience with the horses: "Fill me with your spirit, Lord, that I might lead my horse with a firm hand and a gentle heart." In this prayer,

Marcia, who had never traveled to the Iberian Peninsula or Peru or been involved with horses in any comprehensive way, echoed the sentiments of some of the finest Iberian breeders and equestrians. She beautifully captured the heart and soul not only of the ancient equestrian but the mystic as well.

Like so many others over the years, Marcia found that the flamboyant style of the Peruvian horses allowed her to connect with a side of the horse that may at times be elusive, the divinity implanted within Creation. As we learn to interact with the *imago Dei*, or divine presence, in the horse, we do not worship that animal as a god, but we consciously begin to look for and recognize divine attributes residing within it. Through that process the horse sparks an inner expedition, connecting us with the same divine attributes within ourselves.

In a very real way, horses and humans try to speak to the divinity in each other by intentionally meeting on the holy ground found in the spark of connection between them, a place that is quite beyond exclusively human turf. Holy ground is not a state of bliss but a heightened consciousness and awareness, a growing desire to cultivate inner resources, to embrace the God within.

When a rider approaches a horse in this sacred manner, not only does the horse flourish, but many problems between the horse and the rider also spontaneously, and mysteriously, resolve. Seeing this happen provides humans with a direct experience of the unseen world and how it affects all of our lives.

Living and working with horses in these ways expanded our awareness of Creation and allowed us to experience and enjoy a new dimension of intimacy with it. We were intrigued by the way certain kinds of relationships established between humans and horses helped to unveil the divine presence in both. Looking at our venture in this way shed new light on previous encounters we'd had with the breeders of Iberian horses. Many of the stories we had heard about these animals began to make more sense. We remembered stories of breeders who were willing to put themselves and their families at risk for their love of the horses. In other stories, horses and humans under very stressful circumstances chose to act with dignity and decorum. These stories became increasingly important to us as we found in them further proof of the spiritual connections between humans and horses. A few of these stories are repeated below, and they can easily take on the aura of legends. However, it is important to remember that these events actually occurred in the normal course of everyday life.

NOBLE ACTS

In 1960, Peru instituted what it called agrarian reform, a euphemism for redistributing the wealth. The government removed families from their vast plantations, often at gunpoint, and the land was handed over to untrained workers. Most workers had never managed a farm, and the government's interest in the program proved to be short-lived. Within a brief time, a country that had been rich agriculturally could not feed its own people.

To add insult to injury, a group of terrorists took refuge in the mountains, randomly bombing buildings, raiding farms, and kidnapping successful men and women. They terrorized both rural and urban areas.

The political climate and general upheaval took its toll on many horse breeders, who were for the most part landowners and hardworking agriculturalists. In fact, many lost their lands and homes, and they watched helplessly as their animals were senselessly slaughtered or died from lack of proper care. In spite of the devastation that it caused, the tragic fallout of agrarian reform rarely made the international news.

A breeder we once met, Don Alfredo, related to us the story of how he and his family had to flee their home during the upheaval with only a few hours' notice. Their sole refuge was a friend's ranch in a neighboring country. As they prepared to take only a few personal belongings, the entire family became depressed as they contemplated the fate of their beloved horses, which they had no way to transport with them.

Torn by their difficult choice, they decided to set their horses free. Motivated by their deep love for their animals, the family decided they would take their chances, even against great odds, to run their twenty horses out of the country and over the border to safety. They had mares they couldn't part with and a twenty-five-year-old stallion that had been a fabulous sire and trusted friend. Even at the risk of their own lives, Don Alfredo and his family could not abandon these animals.

While the family was packing, Don Alfredo went out to the barn to have a heart-to-heart talk with his stallion, Moche. He told Moche how grave the situation was and that both human and animal lives were at stake. He begged Moche to stay within range of the trucks that would be carrying the family's belongings, and to make sure that his band of brood mares did the same. Don Alfredo was very concerned because this run to the border would be a difficult, if not impossible, challenge for their aging stallion.

With great anxiety and sadness, Don Alfredo opened the corral doors. At once Moche made contact with the lead mare. They seemed to have a few words. Then Moche took his position at the back of the herd and ran them forward. The family followed the horses in trucks and cars. Moche and the mares ran for three days without rest and with only small rations of food and water. At last, they crossed the border into the next country. By some miracle, they all arrived safely and without incident. Every horse was intact; not a single one had been lost or injured.

Don Alfredo immediately went to care for Moche, to praise him for his courage and a job well done. As soon as the stallion knew his mares were safe and Don Alfredo was pleased, Moche took one last look around and lay down. The heroic horse died that day of a heart attack. It seemed he had held onto life just long enough to fulfill his mission.

Don Alfredo and Moche's story is not unique. Don Luis was another breeder who was caught in the crossfire of agrarian reforms. Over the course of many years, he and El Capitan, his Peruvian stallion, had become loyal companions. The horse was so good-natured that he learned everything very quickly. He knew a wide range of skills, from dressage to reining for the bullring. El Capitan would do anything for Don Luis, and Don Luis would do anything for him.

Then one day Don Luis learned that neighboring farms were being raided and their animals murdered. He feared his ranch would be next. He was beside himself with worry over El Capitan, and he spent many sleepless nights waiting for the worst to happen. He finally confided in his family that he could no longer tolerate the thought of losing El Capitan. They decided, at risk to themselves, to hide El Capitan in their hacienda. El Capitan lived inside the house during the crisis period and was escorted out at night, under the veil of darkness, for exercise and fresh air.

What was amazing about this was that this active and vital ten-year-old stallion, who was accustomed to lots of exercise, the company of other horses, and fresh air, seemed to grasp the seriousness of the situation. He was able to stay quiet and calm in the cramped quarters of the hacienda. He adapted to this foreign way of life out of love. It seemed he truly grasped the ominous potential of the situation and decided to trust Don Luis's judgment completely. Fortunately the plan worked.

Then there is the story of Don Diego, a horse breeder who was imprisoned by terrorists in Peru. Uncertain of his fate, Don Diego needed something to give him hope, and in time his mind was flooded with images of a beautiful herd of horses. He was captivated and inspired by their radiant beauty and proud spirit. If he survived, he knew he needed to continue breeding fine horses. In fact, he felt compelled to do so. Future foals meant life was moving forward. So he began to envision a new breeding program for his ranch.

In his dreams and visions, he instinctively knew which mares to breed to various stallions. As he made these decisions, he saw each colt and filly in his mind's eye. Each foal came into view like a hologram. His ability to visualize became acute. He was so excited by what he envisioned that he became determined to stay alive in spite of the many great hardships of his captivity. He wanted to see the offspring he was envisioning. It was this desire, during his imprisonment, that kept him going.

Ultimately, Don Diego was set free. He immediately put his dreams into action, and a little over a year later, his fantasies began to come to fruition. What he discovered was hard to believe. The things he'd visualized during his captivity were not idle fantasy, for what he had seen in his mind's eye was in fact becoming a reality. The offspring were almost identical to what he had imagined.

From these stories, as well as our experiences with Trianero, we quickly came to appreciate the power of this boundless love between human and horse. These were not just isolated stories of noble acts; they suggested a special bond between horses and humans that was quite extraordinary. We developed an intense desire to learn more about these Peruvian horses and their incredible spirit.

RETURN TO IBERIA

Once we began retracing the roots of the Peruvian horse, we discovered equine traditions deeply rooted in the spiritual, with whole cultures dedicated to the horse. People within these cultures looked for and found imperishable life lessons while spending time with their horses. In our very midst in Spain we found a group of breeders who had continued this tradition of horse-human interactions for centuries. The cultural traditions of Iberia were still very much alive, providing us with living models of an ancient way of life in which deep friendships with horses was the norm, not the exception. Those who maintained these traditions made a deliberate effort to consistently seek the sacred aspects of being that their horses embodied.

Whether the horse had been bred in Spain, Peru, Portugal, Mexico, Puerto Rico, or Colombia, the Iberian signature made itself known in the animal's noble character. It was fascinating to discover that after so many centuries breeders still consciously nurtured the signature characteristics of this horse-human connection. They did this by choosing horses with a more highly developed spiritual sense. This goal became the main thrust of their breeding program, not an afterthought. The Spanish horse was bred, above all else, for its keen mind, courage, dignity, generous disposition, and convergence with humans.

To Iberians, working with horses is a religious endeavor, and as we witnessed the passion in their endeavors, we became convinced we should bring these horses into our own work. They perceive the horse as a direct agent of God, set apart by its ability to transcend its base instincts and transform them into spiritual traits. This distinction is manifest by the equines' capacity to love, forgive, obey, remain loyal, and show tenderness. For Iberians, horses are four-legged prayer, and the example of their lives can guide us toward passionate living.

Learning of this numinous tradition only begat more questions. What other philosophies and unique ideas had these people embraced in their unique relationship to horses? Why did they choose, first and foremost, to breed a horse with so much allure and loyalty, a horse that transformed humans by its very presence? We set out to understand what went into developing the Spanish horse and its many descendants, and why its temperament and character became so extraordinary.

CHAPTER 5

The Celtic Way — A Model for Spiritual Cross-Training

Taming unbridled impulses freed energy, so that the individual could develop higher virtues and gain inner freedom. Working with a powerful steed underneath spurred this transcendence of Ego. Being mounted on a horse was symbolism made manifest.

As time passed during our study of ancient equestrian traditions, the direction of our journey became increasingly evident to us, with new clues revealed almost daily about the ways that horses extend themselves as spiritual guides and teachers. To open ourselves to these dimensions, we realized we would need to stop giving so much power to our Egos and to instead follow a path that emphasized the inherent goodness of the human soul. We started by focusing less attention on our self-esteem, our personal image, and our competency and turning more attention to what was happening in our relationships with the horses, with one another, and with the world around us. As we pursued this path, we had to live for long periods of time without answers or resolution...and sometimes without much success. Slowly, we learned to suspend our frenzy. Even in the early stages of making these changes in our lives — of consciously working on becoming less egocentric, more selfless, and more open-minded — we noticed that our horses were becoming more responsive to us.

Along with these changes, and with the help of the horses, we became increasingly aware of the great chasms, particularly for us moderns, between the human ego and the soul. While we were experiencing changes in ourselves and finding direction from our studies, we had no clear model to follow. We knew no one who might be able to provide us with what we'd begun to refer to as *spiritual cross-training*. The model we hoped to find was one with roots in the ancient past that would help us commune more fully with nature and the animals.

Since we were uncertain of our path and of where to find a model for it, we took the advice of our mare Alicia and returned to church. The reason we were initially reluctant to return to a Christian church was that earlier in our lives we had been disillusioned by it, finding that it offered us little or no spiritual direction. During our fifteen years away from the church, we had turned for guidance to other religious traditions, including Buddhism, Sufism, and Hinduism, and we had learned much from them. Nevertheless, we were determined to follow Alicia's suggestion to learn about communion, even though we had no great expectations about what we'd receive.

One Sunday morning, skeptical but curious, we dragged ourselves off to the local church, only to discover that the parish had a new priest. Prepared for boredom, we were pleasantly surprised to find the new priest's sermon was powerful and exciting. This was not the kind of priest we had known earlier in our lives. To the contrary! This priest reminded us of the Scottish holy man we had met so many years before on our way to the Isle of Mull in the Scottish Hebrides.

As we left the church, we stopped to thank the priest, Father George, and to get acquainted with him. As we talked, the subject of horses arose. Unlike so many other clergy we had met, Father George was excited and genuinely interested to learn that we were using horses for healing. He was not just being polite. Moreover, it was clear from even this short conversation with him that he was not a conformist, simply following the decree of the church. He was very much his own man, as they say, and very direct about his likes and dislikes. He told us he believed animals can and should play a greater role in all aspects of human life, most particularly in religion, as St. Francis had instructed. This belief was certainly the last thing we'd expected or anticipated receiving from church that morning.

We went home that Sunday feeling that Alicia had definitely steered us in the right direction. On the Wednesday following our visit to his church, Father George called and made an appointment to visit our ranch. It was the first of many wonderful visits we would have together. During our initial meeting, he'd spoken of how he'd become a priest, of how he'd received a "calling" at age thirteen. He had accepted that calling, and since that moment his life had been full of surprises.

For example, he was driving home one day after making a visit to a hospital to pray for a man who was dying. Ahead of him on the freeway, a car door suddenly opened and a woman jumped out. Two passing cars hit her. Although several cars away, Father George witnessed the entire tragedy. Naturally, he stopped to provide whatever assistance he could offer. Within minutes, an ambulance arrived and the paramedics pronounced the woman dead. He watched sadly as they placed a body bag over her, leaving one of her hands sticking out.

Moved by a deep sadness, Father George walked over to

give the woman her last rites. He remembers that, in the moment, he was not feeling very spiritual. What he had just seen had unnerved him, and his heart was pounding.

The prayer he uttered for the woman was completely spontaneous. He bent over her body, touched her hand, and spoke to God bluntly and sincerely: "I don't feel very spiritual," he said. "I can't even think of what to say, God, but please help this woman and her family. Do what you can." Moments later, the woman sat straight up.

The crowd was stunned. At first the paramedics were speechless. However, they regained their composure, examined her, and lifted her onto a stretcher. As they were putting her into the ambulance, the woman thanked Father George. He asked if there was anything he could help her with, and she asked for her purse. Her bag had been thrown into the street, yet no one in the crowd had touched it. As he handed the purse to her, he blessed her. Father George had no idea who this woman was, nor did she know him. Yet they had touched each other in a tender and profound way.

As he told this story, we listened intently. What amazed us, besides the event itself, was the absence of any Ego he brought to the telling. He was jovial and humble as he related these miraculous events to us. Clearly, he accepted even such extraordinary occurrences graciously, recognizing that they came from God. In his eyes, healing and wholeness were a normal part of life and nature. To Father George, nothing was out of the ordinary in the metaphysical world of the Divine. And he never questioned that all praise for this miracle belonged to God.

Over the months, as our friendship with Father George grew, he revealed that his delightful view of the world had been deeply influenced by his study of Celtic spirituality. Through him, we gained greater familiarity with these traditions, which reminded us of what we had learned about the Iberian horse community during our travels in Spain. Indeed, Father George was escorting us into the deep wisdom of the ancient traditions we had been seeking, and we could have asked for no better support and guidance.

We learned that many of the earliest Celtic beliefs and customs had been painstakingly preserved and that even today there are many who maintain these mystical traditions. Celtic philosophy drew from both East and West and included Semitic influences. These Celtic ways connect us with the descendants of those original religious horsemen, the equestrians of antiquity whom we had heard about in Spain. We also shared with Father George what we'd learned about the ways the Celts had actively cultivated their distinct tradition of working with animals to improve the human soul.

To the Celtic people, God's Creation was more than a gift. It was a direct divine revelation. They saw God presenting his infinite grace through nature and in nature. All of Creation, in Celtic terms, was a *theophany:* that is, a direct communication from God through the physical manifestation of all and everything. The Celts knew that the Divine Image is literally the heart of the created world. As the Celtic writer John Scotus Eriugena explains, "Creation is not God, but it is angelic, prophetic, revelatory, and through it God speaks."[1]

Our exchanges with Father George reminded us that interacting with animals kept the Celtic people spiritually fit, expansive, and cosmically interactive, providing their culture with a mystical edge rare in Western society. We learned, for example, that the Archangel Michael, the patron saint of horses and the sea, was often summoned by the Celtic people during their life passages, most particularly during conception and death. Women who were unable to bear children would seek the help of St. Michael, as would families experiencing misfortune or in mourning. J. Philip Newell writes, "These 'womb' times and 'tomb' times represented a passing over from the invisible to the visible, or from the seen into the unseen. Similarly he was associated with the end of time when, in the midst of a mighty wind or cosmic fire, a new heaven and earth would be born."[2]

On September 29, an important feast day for the Celts, there would be a morning procession, on horseback, to a burial ground. Later in the day the Celts, both men and women, participated in a wild horse race, riding bareback without bridles. Executing a race on horseback without tack is quite an equestrian feat; it is the ultimate test of one's riding skills. Furthermore, as J. Philip Newell writes: "In preparation for the festivities it was permissible on the Eve of Michaelmas to steal a horse for use on the following day, with the understanding that it was to be returned after the Day of Michael. It was also a day of love-gifts and love-making, with promises and tokens of love exchanged between young men and women. Related to this was the giving and receiving of carrots as symbols of fertility and offspring."[3]

The ancient Celts loved to travel and explore the unknown. They formed caravans and would relocate in bands, taking their households and livestock with them. Sometimes relocation was a practical matter; for example, they moved west after the Ice Age in search of more fertile land. At other times, their wandering does not seem to have been motivated by practicalities as much as by an adventurous spirit. They felt that leaving security behind developed character.

The Celts' idiosyncratic love of travel developed into their passion for making pilgrimages to "thin places." These were places of discovery — such as remote islands, unknown forests and holy lands, and mythical realms like the land of beasts — where humans might catch glimpses of the invisible dimension. Traveling on horseback was particularly important in this endeavor, for the animals were physical and spiritual guides that helped the Celts find and enter the thin places. Clearly, horses in these instances literally brought their riders closer to God. As J. Philip Newell writes, "The figure in the Celtic tradition who is connected most closely with the wildness of creation's elements is the Archangel Michael. He is regarded as the patron saint of the sea and of horses. His name simply means 'One who resembles God.' As angel or messenger of God he is portrayed as riding an unbridled horse in the midst of the wind. The horse and rider are elemental. They ride at the heart of the wind of God."4

Lessons of the Celtic Character

The Celtic people were intellectual, passionate, artistic, and highly imaginative. Due to their robust and holistic attitude toward life, they have a legendary reputation as poet-warriors. This seemingly contradictory persona has perplexed historians over the centuries. However, when examined within the mystical context of their lives, it not only makes sense but gives us clues about the nature of their bonds with horses, perhaps providing us with models to follow in our own work with these animals.

The Celts were poets because of their boundless capacity for love, joy, generosity, and spontaneity. Unlike the secular cultures of today, they gave themselves wholeheartedly to the Infinite. They savored the love of God through every facet of Creation, seeing the world and everything in it as a living icon. The Celts drew, whenever possible, from the imagery within Creation, opening doors to their contemplative stance — which was clearly one of wonder, beauty, and awe. They also used drama and storytelling to captivate the heart and touch the soul.

Recently, one of our clients shared how the Celtic use of imagery, storytelling, and nature can serve us today in modern life. Cindy (not her real name), a famous actress, came for our five-day equine retreat. She was going through an unhappy and difficult divorce at the time. She was feeling shaken when she arrived and had lost some of her characteristic courage.

Since Cindy loved horses, she thought an equine retreat might do her some good. We immediately discovered that she had remarkable communication with horses. In fact, she excelled with them immediately, in part because she was able to focus her attention even though she was quite distraught about her life. We taught her communion with horses through an exercise in which one visualizes the Golden Mare. Here is that exercise:

> You are on your Golden Mare. She loves you and you love her. Both your hearts are open, and you ride to the top of a bright green hill. It is so beautiful today. You know what this mare is saying to you. She is filled with feeling just as you are now. It is quiet, just the two of you. You are like two separate trees whose underground roots are mingling. You dismount. You put your arm around her neck; she feels warm and loving. You are now in the heart of nature, the place of oneness. You stroke the mare; you can smell the sweetness of her skin. You can see her shining golden color. The oneness and healing are complete. Thank God for all your blessings.

Cindy was soothed by this meditation, and so was Alicia, the real "golden mare" she had ridden. By the end of the retreat, Cindy left feeling renewed, her old courage to meet life's challenges fully restored.

Months later Cindy phoned us, telling us about a most wonderful experience she'd had that was related to the Golden Mare exercise. While in New York, she was riding her bicycle and became overcome by fear and doubt. Suddenly she remembered the horses, and in her mind her bike was transformed into the Golden Mare. Cindy and the Golden Mare were one, and this gave her the immediate strength and calm she needed. With the help of the Golden Mare visualization, Cindy drew from the poetry of nature to allay her fears.

If this experience represents the poetic side of Celtic wisdom, what is the warrior side, and how did it figure into the character of these people? We can speculate that they drew warrior strength from nature's demonstrations of volatility and wildness — that is, from the stormy and unpredictable side of Creation.

Whether poets or warriors, the Celts lived passionately. As warriors, they were fierce contenders. The Celtic warrior and the Celtic mystic conjure up notoriously wild images today. Nothing illustrates this better than the tales of great armies of warriors charging into battle nude, their bodies painted blue, and wearing torques, or collars, around their necks. A bard accompanied them on their campaigns, filling them with tall tales and whipping them up into an emotional froth. Many of the men, it was reported, raged into battle with erections. The women also were warriors. Prudence Jones and Nigel Pennick write, "The ancient writers report that the Celtic women were tall, fierce, and strong, and as terrible in battle as their men, and Celtic coins often depict a naked woman on horseback triumphantly brandishing a spear or a sword."[5] One can only imagine these wild, painted warriors thundering against the enemy in all their nude glory. What a sight!

Even though the Celts had an inclination for wildness, they directed these impulses well. They were psychologically adroit and knew that wildness could be used constructively or destructively, depending on how it was applied and for what purpose. J. Philip Newell writes, "The Celtic tradition deeply affirms the unbounded side of life. It seeks a wild naturalness of place and an untamable energy of power. In the prayers of the Hebrides the elemental forces of earth, sea, and sky are recognized as potentially destructive. The goodness of their wild energy, however, is invoked."[6]

While military training shaped the warrior's inner character, the overriding purpose of this training was to teach the warrior to look beyond the immediate present and find peace in the Infinite. The Celts knew that self-indulgence, self-centeredness, and selfish motives, all pervasive human tendencies, were obstacles to their development, were characteristic of overly developed egos, and were humanity's only true enemy. So the warrior worked to develop his self-control and inner strength. Taming unbridled impulses freed energy, so that the individual could develop higher virtues and gain inner freedom. Working with a powerful steed underneath spurred this transcendence of Ego. Being mounted on a horse was symbolism made manifest. The image of Archangel Michael mounted on a horse provided a powerful model. Elevated both physically and emotionally by the power, speed, intelligence, and sheer bulk of the horse, one was carried into the spiritual realm, living closer to one's divine nature. The Celtic warrior was taught always to ride at the center of the wind, for the wind was literally and symbolically God's spirit and breath.

COMMUNION, NOT CONQUEST

The Celtic people would likely have emerged as a greater world power had they been more interested in the tedious task of administration. They shunned excessive organization, management, conformity, and urbanization. They preferred to live in the country, operate in clans, move when they wanted, and have a decentralized political system. They prided themselves on being a cultural organism that served the people, not an institution that enslaved them. They were fiercely opposed to injustice and bureaucracy because of their great love of independence and freedom. In time, due to their lack of management, they were unable to compete with more regimented societies, such as the Roman Empire. Consequently, this once vast and influential civilization was pushed farther and farther to the outer regions of Europe, until the Celts reached their present homeland of Ireland and the British Isles.

We seldom hear much about Celtic spirituality today, but in fact it continues to exist in modern life. This way of living has persisted, but its bastions of faith go largely unnoticed in our industrial world. In retrospect, we now recognize our Scottish shepherd as a guardian of the Celtic faith. Then there are those like Father George, who continue to disseminate the spiritual teachings of these people, allowing us to become familiar with and apply their wisdom in our everyday lives. With an awakened awareness of Celtic ways, we are perhaps better prepared to access the lessons of that creature of God that was the source of so much of their wisdom — the horse.

CHAPTER 6

Celtic Mysticism

The Celts understood that nature triggers a reverence for all of Creation. They lived within a vibrant domain of compassion and intensity. They were agrarian, and milking a cow, tilling a field, riding a horse, or uttering a prayer were to them one and the same. They all required love and devotion. They knew, as did the Desert Fathers and Mothers of Christianity, the experience of traversing the treacherous and ethereal landscapes of our inner and outer topography, where God would reveal Himself. In this journey, one might be distilled and reduced to one's vital essence.

The more we learned, the more the old Scottish shepherd's words came back to us. We seemed indeed to find ourselves on an unexpected spiritual path. By listening to our horse Alicia, we had gone back to church and found Father George, whose teachings about Celtic spirituality enlightened us. Here, at last, was an embodiment of the mystical tradition that had become so important to us in our equine therapy program. Based on harmony and kinship with all of Creation, Celtic spirituality fostered an understanding of the mystery of God, the surrender of self, and the ability of the human heart to embrace the essential goodness of Creation.

The Irish monk Columbanus said that if you wish to know

the Creator, you must come to know his creatures. Kinship with animals had always been an integral part of Celtic beliefs and practices, in both the pagan and Christian eras. It was an entry into a new and more vital communication with God. Since *being religious* meant befriending God, neighbors, friends, animals, the elements, trees, and so on, the Celts were encouraged to make these sacred connections as an essential part of their spiritual lives. Doing so led to an expansive set of beliefs instead of a reductionist one. Theirs emphasized love and understanding instead of judgment and condemnation. Law, sin, dreariness, and austerity were not part of Celtic theology.

A Celtic mystic of the fourth century, Pelagius, said, "God is Love." Pelagius held that infants were born in the image of God and wholly good. One of his famous remarks was, "If you look into the eyes of an infant, you will see the face of God." He believed that God also embraces and includes all peoples and nations, despite church affiliation or religion or race. In other words, whether we go to church or not, or even believe or not, we are all God's creation.

Pelagius adhered to the spirituality and practices of the Desert Mothers and Fathers. The Desert Mothers and Fathers were early Christian mystics who went into the deserts of Egypt, Palestine, Arabia, and Persia around the fourth century A.D. to cultivate their spirituality. He lived close to Christ consciousness and had many dedicated students, both men and women, whom he directed spiritually. He was also a staunch believer in humans taking responsibility for their actions, and not blaming God for their own poor choices. In fact, Pelagius was so inclusive that he educated the women of his day in the Holy Scripture and in religious practices, and because he did so, he was ostracized by the authorities of the early Christian church in Rome. Pelagius was eventually branded a heretic because of his progressive views by his contemporary St.

Augustine of Hippo, father of the Roman Church and forerunner of subsequent reformationist doctrines within the Western church. By contrast, Augustine's dogma was dualistic, antiwomen, antianimal, bureaucratic, and based upon his famous construct of original sin. The Western church and our society would be very different today if St. Augustine had not silenced Pelagius. Pelagius, once censored, retreated to the desert of Egypt and died approximately two years later.

According to Pelagius, we can know only that mystery exists, but we can't know the mystery. Its magnitude is beyond comprehension because God is transcendent, immanent, and inconceivable. Love and education, according to this inspiring Celtic theologian, were both portals into knowing that this vast realm of unknowing exists.

In the introduction to his collection of Pelagius's letters, editor Robert Van de Weyer states, "Pelagius also stressed the sanctity of all God's creation. He regarded the beauty of nature as a reflection of God's beauty, and he urged people to care for animals and even plants for their own sake."[1]

Even after the Celts embraced Christianity, they considered animals to be their partners and spiritual guides. To the Celts, every creature was invested with spirit, mystery, and energy. We have learned this firsthand with our own horses; merging with an animal, and experiencing its energy, invigorates our lives, awakens our energetic centers, our chakras, and becomes a way to experience our own sentient nature and our creatureliness in God's Creation.

"What is manifested," writes J. Philip Newell, "is an expression of God's essence. Nothing in creation exists in and by itself. The soul of every creature is derived from the one Soul. God, therefore, is not simply in every creature but is the essence of every creature. At heart, creation — including our creatureliness — is a showing forth of the mystery of God."[2]

The Celts named animals individually and treated them as members of the family or clan. Intimate involvement in the animal world did not separate them from God; rather, it brought them closer because they understood that Creation was linked to the mystery of Christ and the incarnation.

The Celtic Christian Era

St. Patrick converted Ireland to Christianity in the fifth century, and he did so without spilling one drop of blood. Patrick did what others can only dream of today: he converted the entire island peacefully. One reason for Patrick's success was that the Celts had been anticipating Christ long in advance; they had even prophesied his coming incarnation. Consequently, they readily accepted his teachings. But Christ's mandate to "Love thy neighbor as thyself" had wider implications for them. They applied it not just to other human beings but to everything in the physical world.

Since the Celts embraced the cosmic vision of Christ, they accentuated this facet of the religion. The cosmic Christ was the man who calmed the storm, brought fish out of the sea, and cursed the fig tree. They cemented this bond by living in nature and reading the sacred texts in a unique way. They paid attention to the land and to the seasons. This embrace of nature has continued into modernity, and making a nature or wilderness quest is central to their theology.

No doubt of equal importance to the Celtic preparedness for Christianity was the fact that the brand of Christianity that Patrick brought to Ireland had not yet been excessively colored by the dictates and political overtones of the Roman Empire. Patrick's religion retained its roots in Middle Eastern mysticism, philosophy, psychology, and the cosmology of the desert.

The Celts understood that nature triggers a reverence for all of Creation. They lived within a vibrant domain of compassion and intensity. They were agrarian, and milking a cow, tilling a field, riding a horse, or uttering a prayer were to them one and the same. They all required love and devotion. They knew, as did the Desert Fathers and Mothers of Christianity, the experience of traversing the treacherous and ethereal landscapes of our inner and outer topography, where God would reveal Himself. In this journey, one might be distilled and reduced to one's vital essence.

The Celts communicated with God in two key ways — through communion with Creation and through the Bible. Most Christian traditions today, except for some of the Catholic and Anglican communities reclaiming their Celtic roots, ignore Celtic connections with nature and rely only on the Bible. The Protestant traditions most often defer all inner authority to the literal Word and leave nature out of their spiritual paradigm. Hence, they keep the Word entombed. In Greek, "word" is *logos,* best understood as eternal and esoteric wisdom, the immutable Truth.

It's important to understand that the Celts did not abandon nature in favor of studying the Word, nor did they abandon Scripture in favor of nature's teachings. Rather, they sought a balance between the two, believing they could achieve spiritual maturity in this way. The Celts always sought wholeness and balance; direct spiritual experience was as invaluable as the lessons of Scripture. In the Celtic spiritual paradigm, nothing was either/or; it was always both/and. They believed that God likes to reveal Himself in all mediums, and one way without the other was limiting.

ANIMALS AND SAINTS

Unlike other western Christians, the Celts never ceased to be involved with nature. Many of the relationships the Celtic mystics had with animals and the land attest to this fact.

St. Cuthbert, a seventh-century Celtic saint of Northumbria, would let the otters dry his feet. John Marsden in *The Illustrated Bede* relates the following story: "Cuthbert went down to the sea-shore beneath the monastery; and going deep into the water until the swelling waves rose up to his neck and arms, he spent the dark hours of the night watching and singing praises accompanied by the sound of the waves. When dawn approached he went on to the land and again began to pray, kneeling on the shore. As he did so, there at once came out from the depths of the sea two four-footed creatures which are commonly called otters. Stretching themselves out in front of him on the sand, they began to warm his feet with their breath and sought to dry him on their fur. Having performed their services, they received his blessing and slid back beneath the waves in which they lived."3

St. John of Beverley, a Celtic saint in northern England, also loved animals. Marsden writes, "The last of John's miracles recorded by Bede tells of a horse race held by students accompanying the saint on his travels and John's premonition and healing of an injury to one of the young horsemen. Bede recalls how he learned of the miracle from the man himself, the priest Herebald."4

St. Columba, one of the most revered Celtic saints, was a sixth-century Irish monk who founded many monasteries in Ireland and on Iona. As the story goes, St. Columba was told of his coming death by his horse. Perhaps moved by compassion, sorrow, or an overwhelming gratitude for his master, the horse perceived a transition; he was chosen to bid his master farewell and help him pass from this world to the next. When the horse rested his head on Columba and wept, Columba realized it would soon be his own time to die. Columba comforted the horse and thanked him for being such a loyal and faithful friend. This warning gave Columba a rare opportunity to prepare for his death and to say good-bye to others.

St. Melangell, another Celtic saint, was the daughter of an Irish king. Melangell was given a portion of land in Wales after God gave her the ability to protect the wild hare from some unruly hunting dogs. According to Nigel Pennick in *The Celtic Saints,* "After that, the lands of Pennant Melangell became a sanctuary under her guardianship. She lived there for another thirty-seven years, during which time no animal was killed on her land.... St. Melangell is recognized today as the Celtic patroness of animals and the natural environment. According to the Celtic Christian philosophy, because the natural environment is the manifestation of God's will on earth, those who would destroy it are not only threatening the continuance of all life on earth, but are also going counter to *the protection and favor of the Creator.*"[5]

Each of these stories gives us but a hint of the powerful and intimate connection between animals and the Celtic saints, and of the role animals played in their spiritual lives. Animals taught the saints about the delight, sorrow, and reality of being a creature. Even in modern times, the Celtic people still practice shape-shifting. Shape-shifting is the ancient shamanic art in which a person sheds his or her human identity to become an animal, thus melding with Creation. In that respect, this practice is a form of communion. It is a great exercise of the imagination, often marking the beginning stages of the mystical quest, where one experiences dimensions of our existence that extend beyond the mundane.

Exploring the Inner Self

If we truly want to discover our own obstacles to personal and spiritual development, the Celts suggested that we should explore our inner self. They advocated examining our personal prejudices — what we are for, what we are against — and using nature to aid us in this process. Through their experiences with nature, the Celts learned a kind of humility and appreciation for the great vastness of Creation that could not be conveyed with words alone. For example, they learned through this intimate connection with all creatures that judgments, even if valid, consume energy and prevent clarity of thought and transcendence. In modern psychotherapeutic language, we might say that unneutralized energy prevents growth and inventiveness.

The stories that follow are examples of how judgments and narrow-mindedness cause spiritual imbalance. They show how the judgmental mind, even when seemingly justified, eventually interferes with our growth and transformation. They are also examples of how horses communicate to us about this, whether we choose to listen to these communications or not.

Martha was a spiritual teacher who came to work with us because she was having problems with her mare, who was bucking off Martha continually. Martha said she wanted help controlling her horse and handling her own and the horse's fear. After a few lessons, it became obvious to us that Martha did not realize or want to acknowledge her own responsibility for her horse's reaction to her. She wanted the problem solved, but she was not interested in admitting her part in it or ultimately in developing a better relationship with her horse.

While it was true that her mare was aggressive, Martha chose to dismiss all the signs pointing to her own inability to cultivate a harmonious relationship with the animal. Instead of examining herself and trying to discern what the mare might be revolting against, Martha only blamed the horse. Indeed, she considered herself a mystic and made much of her reputation as a spiritual guru who could communicate with animals. She believed that she talked with animals, and they with her, and considered herself a great lover of nature. Despite what was happening in her relationship with her mare, she continued to flaunt her abilities, demonstrating that she would rather discount the obvious than jeopardize this version of herself.

Wanting to appeal to her self-image as a spiritual person, we asked her one day if she ever read the Bible, or the Vedas, or the Koran, or other spiritual texts. We thought perhaps we could appeal to her through one of these teachings. She responded, "I don't need that stuff. I already know it. I am too far beyond that. I just love nature."

Frankly, we were stunned by Martha's arrogance. We could only imagine what her mare must feel. For us, true spirituality is always inclusive; it never discounts teachings from other belief systems or paradigms. This comment revealed to us what Martha's mare was reacting to — her supercilious attitude, her pride. The mare refused to trust Martha because Martha failed to work toward gaining more purity of heart or depth of character. Martha did not have enough humility to lay her own Ego needs aside and truly love her horse. She did not realize that in order to lead her horse, she needed to be humble before it. In spite of whatever good intentions Martha had, she was unconsciously avoiding the often painful process of exploring her own character and surrendering her will. Martha surrendered to no one. She never became a horsewoman, and she ultimately gave the mare away.

Another client, Susan, came to us because she adored horses but suffered from anxiety attacks every time she tried to ride. She had grown up in a poor family in East Germany. Upon immigrating to the United States, she had worked very hard and, as she told us, "overcome my station in life." We thought this was an odd remark for such a polished professional. She had earned her degree in law, was financially well off, and was a leader in the community. Her fear of riding just didn't make sense because in all other ways she was very competent, and she appeared to us as very spiritual, gracious, and loving.

Then one day we were discussing the Spanish Riding School and its tradition, and Susan went up in smoke. Her eyes darted back and forth like daggers, and she launched into a diatribe about the injustices of the bourgeois. Susan's rage came out of the blue; it was completely out of character. We listened but made no comment. As time went on, her attitude toward the Spanish Riding School softened because she discovered that its wisdom about horses gave her more understanding and confidence. Shortly thereafter, her riding vastly improved and her fear began to diminish.

However, as Susan progressed and became a better rider, she began avoiding her lessons. She had one excuse after another. Everything seemed to interfere with her riding time. We waited, knowing her love for horses would override her fears.

Then several weeks later Susan arrived in a huff. As she mounted her horse, she commented that she could not believe that a proletarian (referring to herself) would adore any method born from the minds of the aristocracy. Listening to her own words, she herself was stunned. She even reflected on how immature she sounded, and how hypocritical. She had always thought of herself as being free of prejudices.

As Susan became conscious of this inner conflict, she began to understand what stood in the way of her riding. In her mind the horse symbolized class distinction, and this struck the place in her psyche where she still felt inferior. Turning to horses, for Susan, was like joining the enemy.

Susan realized that, in her heart, she had not yet transcended her early self-image and ideology — what she had called her *station in life*. She still saw the world as an ongoing conflict between proletarian and aristocrat, and this prevented her from obtaining a unity of spirit. Anthony DeMello, the wonderful and wise Jesuit priest and psychologist, used to say,

"God makes the sun shine on Saints and Sinners." In Susan's case, that sun shone on proletarians and aristocrats. As long as Susan held on to these prejudices, she would limit how far she could grow, both with horses and in her own joy. Susan worked through her prejudices and became increasingly aware.

Conversely, the Celtic mystics provide wonderful, ideal models of how a high level of spiritual integration can affect one's life. The example of the Celtic mystic Cuthbert shows us what kind of harmony can happen when one is free of prejudice. Cuthbert freed himself from pretense and social position until his only identity was as a creature of God. He was well grounded in nature, and he followed God's will. Since he did not limit himself by overidentifying with a group or playing roles, Creation accepted him readily. As John Marsden describes, "Not only did the creatures of the air minister to the venerable man, but so too did sea animals and indeed the sea itself. For if a man serves the Author of all Creation faithfully and with all his heart, it is no wonder that every creature should defer to his command and wishes. Yet we in general lose control of the creation that is subject to us because we neglect to do service in our turn to the Lord and Creator of all things. The very sea, as I say, was quick to minister to Christ's servant when he had need."[6]

This outlook provides the opportunity to bring the eternal world closer, unifying the visible with the invisible. As John O'Donohue writes in *Anam Cara,* "We have falsely specialized the eternal world. We have driven the eternal out into some kind of distant galaxy. Yet the eternal world does not seem to be a place but a different state of being."[7]

As a result of their holistic, nature-based philosophy, the Celtic contemplatives felt a broad kinship with other mystics. They had a universal affiliation with what the late Thomas Merton, a modern contemplative, called the Church of the

Desert, a spiritual locale that transcends culture, time, and space. This could be any environment where the two worlds of the Divine and the temporal meet. This is also a sacred space where our consciousness is transformed.

Merton advocated practical methods of spirituality for true transformation and enlivening the spirit. He wrote, "Very often, the inertia and repugnance which characterize the so-called *spiritual life* of many Christians could perhaps be cured by a simple respect for the concrete realities of everyday life, for nature, for the body, for one's work, one's friends, one's surroundings, etc. A false supernaturalism which imagines that the *supernatural* is a kind of Platonic realm of abstract essences totally apart and opposed to the concrete world of nature, offers no real support to a genuine life of meditation and prayer. Meditation has no point and no reality unless it is firmly rooted in life."[8]

THE ORGANIC WAY

The Celts chose the Gospel of John as their favorite scripture, primarily for its mystical content. They loved the Gospel of John so much that many of them memorized it. They believed that John clearly spelled out our proper relationship to God and the universe. In the biblical story of the vine and the branches, we learn how humans can thrive and reach their full potential. St. John is very clear in his intent: only by staying connected to the vine can we flower and bear fruit, and in order to flower we will face periods of darkness and pruning. In this metaphorical story, John quotes Jesus as saying, "I am the true vine, and my Father is the vinedresser. Every branch in me that bears no fruit, he cuts away, and every branch that does bear fruit he prunes to make it bear even more. You are pruned already, by means of the word that I have spoken to you. Make your home in me, as I make mine in you. As a branch cannot bear fruit all by itself, but must remain part of the vine, neither can you unless you remain in me" (John 15:1–4; Jerusalem Bible).

The Celts found in this gospel the foundation for their belief that living a spiritual and productive life is simple. When the branches are severed from the root, our lives decay; as long as we stay connected to the root, living our lives through divine guidance, we grow and thrive. As a Sufi master put it, "To be under divine Grace and guidance means to realize your connection with the Essence which gave emanation to all life. If you don't recognize this connection, your efforts will be confined to the limitations of your individual existence as separate from the Cosmic Whole, and this is *occultism*."[9] As this growth occurs, we need to recycle it. We must use our potential and talents for the benefit of others. The Gospel of John thus helps us to understand that true spirituality is an unending cycle of feeding and being fed, in which selfish consumerism has no part. Sometimes it takes an ordeal — such as the challenge that horses sometimes provide us in our relationships with them — to make us realize what our priorities need to be.

The Celts wholeheartedly embraced the idea of living within a spiritual ecosystem, obeying the divine hierarchy. In short, they took orders from above, carefully nurturing their wisdom to detect this inner divine voice. They were ever-conscious that our identity is as creature, not Creator, and if we want access to the unlimited perceptions and resources of the Divine, we must commune with the Creator on a continual basis. To do so we need to leave our judgments behind. We can enjoy the pleasures of life, but we are incapable of second-guessing God. Our minds are three-dimensional and finite; God's is holographic and limitless. The Celts' work with horses reminded them of this ever-present reality — that we must maintain our proper place in the Cosmos and stay out of the Creator's business. Considering all of this, it has become abundantly clear to us that if horse work is to be effective and pure, it must be imbued with reverence and respect, and subsumed under the umbrella of God.

While the rest of the Christian world evolved, Celtic spirituality remained virtually unchanged over the centuries. It stayed grounded in the original desert tradition of Jesus. Even today, it is very similar to many of the Middle Eastern practices of the Sufi mystics, who grew out of a similar religious ideology.

We have come to understand that religion in the twenty-first century is not what it used to be. Religion, especially that of the early Celtic Christians, had a very different flavor than it does today. It spoke to a longing deeply embedded in the human heart, and in order to awaken this intrinsic wisdom of the heart, one must regain a connection with nature, even if it is only periodic. We have discovered this reality firsthand while living and working with horses, and within an agrarian lifestyle, for over twenty years.

Studying the ancient Celtic traditions both points to what our relationships with the horses may teach us and affirms what we learn from them. In an age when we increasingly find ourselves distanced from nature, and insulated from the reality of ourselves as creatures and not the Creator, these lessons may literally be our salvation.

CHAPTER 7

Living Close to the Vine

We've discovered that the mystic path is not just about peak experiences, but that, more importantly, it draws from the entire range of life experiences. It is about faithfulness even in the midst of despair. We've learned why the sacred vow is required on the path of the mystic, for it leaves no room to escape the challenges we encounter along the way.

When we first began breeding Peruvian horses, we moved to the Napa Valley and began raising grapes as well, so as to fully immerse ourselves in nature. We went ahead full throttle. For years we were involved in animal husbandry, farming, and psychotherapy.

This immersion gave us a chance to live in the environment in which horses spend most of their time, a way of life with a distinct pace, a distinct set of rhythms and priorities. We wanted to understand this world, feeling it was a way to enhance our inner lives and imagination.

In the process of tending our vines, we had the opportunity to garner many truths about horses and life. Doing psychospiritual therapy in this rural environment, we learned about the mystic way as well. We lived according to nature — following the rhythm of its seasons, births, disasters, and deaths — and experienced firsthand the age-old dictum of life as an unbroken circle.

For the Celts, the circle had mystical properties because it symbolized the cycle of life, death, and rebirth. It was also a reminder that we, too, are a part of nature, equal to other animals and other living things, and equal to one another. Living in the circle places us all in a universal community whose truths supersede sociopolitical hierarchies.

Those who work the land with love are no longer outside the natural chain of life but become an intimate part of it. Individuals who farm or engage in agricultural enterprises because it is a passion first and a business second develop a distinct consciousness, one that mirrors what the mystics call *mindfulness*. You learn to not exploit the land or the animals because you recognize the interconnectedness that brings us all into contact with the sacred. You learn that your ultimate destiny is not self-directed but guided by the Source.

From Grapes to Wine —
Cultivating Our Interior

Though we no longer live in California, our agrarian life there continues to serve as a living metaphor for the process of interior transformation based on the rhythms of nature. Then as now, if our timing is off, we get vinegar instead of wine. We remember how the rhythms of our lives changed with the seasons, and how we shared these changing rhythms with all life around us.

Each year the horses loved the harvest as much as we did. They enjoyed the cooler weather. They also looked forward to eating the ripened grapes as special treats. During harvest season, typically in October, there were many celebrations. There were lively festivities and local fairs often reminiscent of a medieval village. There was always a robust and merry feeling in the air. Harvest is a time of abundance, exhilaration, and thanksgiving.

Harvest is also a sensual time. The aroma of newly pressed grapes wafts through the air. New wine and onion cakes are some of the delectable harvest delicacies. The gondolas clang, making their yearly pilgrimage up and down the wine roads lined with oak trees festooned with Spanish moss. The leaves on the vines are turning vibrant gold and crimson.

By January, all the leaves have fallen. It is time for pruning. The leafless vines, tied crucifixion-style, appear stark and bare, but hold an aura of mystery. Once the vines are barren, we prune deeply in an effort to insure maximum fruit production for the next year. The pruning reroutes the energy of the vine. We cultivate the vines to make fruit, not just greenery, and many of the workers turn this task into a contest. They compete to see who can get the maximum fruit the following season by their special pruning techniques. The canes and other cuttings from the vines are piled and burned. It is time for the grapes to sleep.

During the winter season the vines are dormant. They are fertilized, the earth around them is turned, everything is made ready for spring. Then, miraculously, each spring the vines awaken. As they come into leaf, they turn vibrant green, and mustard begins to grow plentifully between their trunks. The valley becomes a living canvas for nature's art, reminding everyone how glorious and enigmatic life can be. Springtime is jubilant. The whole valley awakens with the excitement of new life emerging. Spring is the time of hope and vigils of rejoicing. The earth becomes a gift; we behold new life, light emerging from darkness, winter quietude giving way to pulsating promise. In this atmosphere of anticipation, we patiently watch and wait. We stand by and tend to the vines, making certain they are healthy and free of insects and disease.

As spring gives way to summer, there isn't much to do but be patient and observant and rest. In the summer season, grapes simply mature. They do not even need much watering. There is a saying in the valley — the grapes like to suffer. Grapes overwatered and babied do not develop as intense a flavor as those that have struggled. They need careful attention, but attention from afar. We become watchful parents. We learn not to interfere but to be available if needed. Maturing grapes need our help only if the temperature becomes too extreme or they become infested. Otherwise they do very well on their own.

The winemaker typically monitors their maturity. He or she oversees their sugar content, and religiously follows the weather to make sure the grapes do not overheat. We stay vigilant because if there is an unexpected rainfall, the ripening grapes must be picked before they burst open. Before long, as the fruit reaches its optimal sugar content, a person with exceptional taste buds will often be designated to sleep in the vineyard, sampling grapes every few hours to determine when they taste just right. It is this connoisseur who makes the judgment call about when the grapes are ready to pick. His or her call is like that of the muezzin from the minaret, who tells the people to turn toward Mecca for prayer. The crier intones aloud, bidding the faithful to come. The vineyard workers ready themselves for the call. When it comes, they put aside whatever they are doing to pick the grapes. Droves of pickers flood the vineyard, day or night, holidays or weekends. Every-one knows it is time to make haste. Through this process, every-one learns to follow nature's time instead of their own. Many lives are rearranged and disrupted during harvest season, but it is well worth it.

LESSONS FROM THE SPIRITUAL ECOSYSTEM

After living in this fashion, we realized that the ways of the mystic, equestrian, and farmer are parallel journeys. Each of these pursuits requires discipline, tradition, rigor, and development of character. Evelyn Underhill, a British mystic, tells us that we have to resurrect a part of our consciousness that has been left fallow: "We hear much of the mystical temperament, the mystical vision. The mystical character is far more important and its chief ingredients are courage, singleness of heart and self-control. It is towards the perfecting of these military virtues, not to the production of a pious softness, that the discipline of asceticism is largely directed; and the ascetic foundation, in one form or another, is the only enduring foundation of a sane contemplative life."[1]

Pursuits such as farming and animal husbandry have historically been likened to the mystical quest. Christopher Bamford reflects: "Just as being born of a virgin the Word became flesh, so too he incarnated in the letters of the scripture and the varied forms of the visible universe. St. Anthony, the Desert Father, when asked, 'How do you ever manage to carry on, deprived as you are of the consolation of books?' replied, 'My book, sir philosopher, is the nature of created things, and that is always at hand when I wish to read the words of God.' Thus we find the equivalence between nature and scripture. The Word is equally present in both and both are in equal measure words of God. Both are signs or gestures evoking principles. Both evoke meaning and permit realization."[2]

In all three endeavors, farming, raising animals, and deepening one's contemplative life, there are many common threads and much shared wisdom. The monks were great farmers, including Brother Mendel, the first geneticist. Mendel knew that we learn more about God's ways by gaining knowledge of the created world. Bamford continues, "Implicit here is the sacramental view that all knowledge is revelation, a perfectly modulated interpenetration of humanity and grace, nature and supra-nature. To the person in the Word, in whom the Word is the person, the Word in the universe speaks. He speaks in the heart. Mountain, grasses, and trees become his Gospels, clouds and animals his prophets."[3]

Devotion and perseverance are most important because without them we cannot handle the inevitable unpredictability and upheaval. The farmer in a good year can reap many benefits, but what happens during drought, pestilence, or floods? Those, too, he must accept with grace. The same is true for those on a spiritual journey. These same lessons in acceptance are evident in breeding horses. Most of the time there is unspeakable joy. However, there is also tragedy.

Natural Upheaval

Carmen, one of our favorite show mares, was expecting her third foal, and we were all very excited. Carmen was a big, beautiful chestnut and a real people-lover. Her previous foals had been easy, fifteen-minute deliveries. Then one night our ranch manager came and knocked urgently on our door. He was very upset. Carmen was having some problems with her delivery. We quickly went down to help her, but the baby was lodged. We tried to reposition the foal, but it was impossible. We called the vet, and he said to wait until he arrived. He explained that if the baby wouldn't easily shift, something was seriously wrong. Moving the foal could kill them both. Carmen grunted and groaned, and we tried to comfort her. Watching our favorite mare suffer was agonizing for us all.

There was nothing we could do but wait by Carmen's side and attempt to comfort her. Looking for assurance, she put her head in our laps, and we stroked her. It was a very difficult situation because we knew she was in both physical pain and emotional anguish, having to watch her baby die. We were doubly worried because we could see she was getting weak and starting to go into shock. Twenty minutes seemed like two hours.

By the time the vet drove onto the property, the foal had died. The vet needed to work quickly because Carmen was failing. She couldn't move the dead foal out of the birth canal. Something had gone terribly wrong in the delivery process. The baby's legs were crosswise in the birth canal. The vet said that what happened was a freak of nature. In moments like this, we learned what it means to surrender to the vast power and incomprehensible wisdom inherent in nature.

The vet told us the procedure for removing the foal would be gruesome and asked if we wanted to leave. We said absolutely not, for we loved Carmen. We would never consider abandoning her for the sake of avoiding the horror she would have to suffer. So we endured the procedure with her; the foal had to be sawed in half. We stayed beside our beloved mare as the vet carefully removed the foal's body parts from the birth canal.

Once the dead foal was extracted, the vet was concerned about infection. So we watched Carmen day and night. We took turns sleeping in the barn with her. Thankfully, she did not get an infection, but we had more work to do.

When she was out of the woods physically, our real work began. Carmen was in great emotional turmoil. She would look all around, calling and crying for her baby. Her eyes were listless, and her head hung low. It was heart-wrenching to see her in such despair. She had always been such a proud and majestic mare. Understandably, she was depressed about the ordeal and needed to go through a grieving process. We could see she wasn't going to bounce back overnight. Her grief and depression continued for months.

During her mourning, she stared blankly and isolated herself. The other mares knew she was distraught, and many tried to comfort her. But Carmen remained aloof. She couldn't seem to shake her loss and grief. All any of us could do was wait patiently and remind her of how much she was loved.

We did try working her under saddle in the hopes of lifting her spirits, but her heart wasn't in it. We held onto our faith and tried to maintain the hope that her spirit would return, but after months it began to seem like wishful thinking. It felt as though we had lost not only the baby but also our beloved Carmen.

We were at the end of our rope. As near as we could tell, Carmen wasn't responding to anyone. Then one day, feeling melancholy ourselves, we walked out to the barn for our morning visit. Much to our surprise, Carmen was eagerly waiting for us. She jumped in the air, let out a joyous whinny, and put on a big show for us. We were ecstatic. Carmen had completed her dark night of mourning and was rejoining the living. Our commitment to Carmen had paid off!

Carmen made a complete physical and psychological recovery, but her days of having foals were over. Recognizing her loss and knowing how much she enjoyed mothering, we decided to give her a new role. We put her in charge of many of our human kids. In time, she became one of our most capable healing horses. Perhaps it was through her own experience of loss and grief that she was able to empathize with others who were having a difficult time. She took a special interest in all youngsters, both human and animal, and extended to them her caring nature. Carmen went on to lead a productive, fulfilling, happy, and healthy life. The kids adored her, and many of them rode her to wins in shows for juniors.

Experiences like the one with Carmen teach us the spiritual way is not always about feeling elated. Neither is it about personal success, effectiveness, or glory. It is about being tenacious and optimistic, even when the odds seem to be clearly against us. It requires an ever-deepening sense of responsibility, faith, and dedication, and is ultimately character enhancing. It requires an ability to stay with a trial because we are invested in the entire process, not just the end result. Similarly, Carmen's experience of losing her baby deepened her in a way that became reflected in her work with the kids.

The mystic and the farmer must be immersed in their processes, be it farming or the contemplative life, from beginning to end. It is each person's responsibility to decide what to cultivate, how to till the soil, how to prepare the ground, when and what to plant, when to weed, water, fertilize, and prune. One must follow the crop until it is time for harvest. By assuming this amount of authority and involvement, we are literally molded by the experience, eventually becoming men and women for all seasons. Even after the harvest, a farmer's work continues. He or she begins to replenish and replant. Being dependent upon the good earth and weather leaves everyone more humble. We come to the stark awareness that the ultimate outcome is not our call but God's.

Every time a crop is destroyed, a calf is born dead, or lightning hits a generator, the farmer or mystic grieves. However, he or she doesn't grovel. By transcending feelings of victimization, individuals find a deeper strength in the center of their beings that underlies their own human emotion and feeling. However, one typically reaches that place only by sheer will. Through this deliberate strengthening of character, one learns poise and endurance. Through weathering the experiences of life, the mystic gains increasing inner composure and calm.

We've discovered that the mystic path is not just about peak experiences, but that, more importantly, it draws from the entire range of life experiences. It is about faithfulness even in the midst of despair. We've learned why the sacred vow is required on the path of the mystic, for it leaves no room to escape the challenges we encounter along the way.

ORDEALS THAT HELP US EXPAND

Horses prune back our Egos and bring us in contact with spirit. They keep us going in the mystic process, even at those times when we may feel reduced. Horses entice us into the realm of the Divine, guided by grace and spirit. Then, once immersed, we are subjected to a process of ongoing pruning, which is beyond our control. In viticulture we prune faithfully for more fruit. Even a thriving and healthy vine gets pruned. We want every vine to reach its potential, and so it is with us.

Once we embark on the mystical path, we are cut back even when we feel we do not want to grow or become more aware. Despite our own selfish assessments of our lives, God and the horse, in unison, push us in a direction we may have never expected or planned. We are met with ordeals that may shake our foundations, threatening all that we once felt we had attained.

By following where the horse leads us emotionally and spiritually, we begin to expand our view of life. Horses give humans a broader perspective on life in general. They give us a keener appreciation of how intelligent and sensitive other creatures are, and this helps develop our own humility and compassion. There are few anecdotes that illustrate this process better than the following one.

Carlin was a teenage client who chronically ran away from home and lived on the streets. Sometimes she would land in a group home, but it never lasted very long. She was hypersensitive to hypocrisy; for example, she would get outraged when a staff member said one thing and did another. When Carlin felt things were unjust, she would blow up verbally or create chaos for everyone around her. Since she had had very little parental guidance, she couldn't handle rules and lacked any sense of inner discipline. She was bitter about life and had stopped listening to anyone or anything. These aspects of her character prevented her from enjoying success in virtually any area of her life. We met Carlin when she was failing in another group program. Since she was running out of options, she volunteered to participate in our horse program.

One day, she pressed us to let her ride Alicia. Initially, we objected because we knew she was not an easy horse to ride for less advanced riders. However, as we listened, we decided that perhaps riding Alicia was not such a bad idea. Alicia's bold spirit might be just the medicine that Carlin needed. We knew she had the equestrian skills to handle the horse (she had learned them from us), but we didn't know if she had developed enough humility or understanding.

We finally decided to let her test her wings because we had confidence and a deep sense of love for Carlin and Alicia. Even if the ride proved to be an ordeal, we believed the experience would be productive. It tested our own faith and our ability to let go. We had to practice what we espouse; goodness would prevail.

Alicia, you will remember, is the mare who advised that if we were to learn communion, we would have to return to church. An elegant mare whom most people loved, she definitely had charisma, was very flashy, and caught everyone's eye. We guessed that Carlin's sudden interest in riding the horse was self-centered. Like many teenagers, Carlin wanted to show off because a video was being made at our place.

Once Carlin mounted, she began to think twice. She discovered that Alicia was very sensitive and did not like being overly controlled. Within a matter of minutes, Carlin could sense Alicia's power. Out of fear, Carlin started to pull on the bit, forgetting all her previous lessons. She had been repeatedly warned to not pull on a horse's mouth with the bit.

As soon as Alicia felt the restraint, she began to accelerate and run full speed ahead. Up to that point, Carlin assumed she knew more than she did, but she was getting a rude awakening. Carlin's attention had been one-sided: she liked lessons on how to animate horses but tuned out the lessons on slowing and stopping because they were "boring."

Now Carlin was discovering how little she knew about Alicia. She had concocted so many fantasies about her own capabilities that she never bothered to ask about Alicia's likes and dislikes.

Alicia took off running, and Carlin began to scream. She kept yelling, "I want to get off." However, that was not an option anymore. Alicia flew around the arena, and all Carlin could do was hang on for dear life. We told her to stop wrenching Alicia's mouth and to stop screaming, but by this time she was too frightened to hear us.

Meanwhile, we knew what Alicia was doing. She was trying to scare Carlin. Alicia had a method of her own for dealing with tough kids. Her plan proved very effective. Alicia just kept running until Carlin released the pressure on the bit and stopped squeezing Alicia's sides. When Carlin stopped manhandling her and softened slightly, Alicia behaved in a very manageable way. Alicia was trying to tell Carlin not to control her by force; she wanted Carlin to use some finesse.

We sensed that Alicia wasn't done with Carlin quite yet. Carlin, except when afraid, refused to control herself and gain inner poise. Instead, she favored forcing and controlling the horse. Carlin didn't ask Alicia politely; she demanded. She expected obedience from the horse without earning it.

When Carlin discovered that the mare was as determined

as she was, she insisted on riding a different horse. We flatly refused, and asked her to remain on Alicia. We knew Carlin needed to work through the challenge that Alicia presented to her, and we thought it was time for her to put her tough-girl skills to some good use. We had her visualize that she was running with a dangerous gang on the streets. This visualization was not very far removed from her own experience.

We asked what she would do on the streets. Carlin told us that on the streets she played it cool, even when her heart was racing. She also tried not to act bossy. These were the skills that would help her to ride Alicia, and even though she was still ambivalent about continuing, Carlin agreed to try one more time.

However, as Carlin rode Alicia again, we could see her getting frustrated and angry. Carlin hadn't put two and two together or truly listened. She was still gripping and not trusting the horse.

Alicia finally reached her breaking point. Instead of running as she did earlier, Alicia reared up on her two hind legs and went straight up into the air. Carlin was terrified, to say the least. And this time, she was too scared to scream.

As Alicia stood on her hind legs, we held our breath. What happened next stunned us. Carlin leaned forward and held on. She did everything by instinct and reacted in the same way a professional would have. She remained calm, went into a forward position, released the bit, and tried to soothe the mare. When Alicia eventually came back down, they both landed together safely.

We walked over to Carlin to ask how she was feeling, and she blurted out, "Did you see that? It was the most awesome experience of my life!" Carlin then told us what had happened. She said that she had had nothing to hang onto and so in sheer terror had just asked for God's help. When she finally let go, she saw a huge orange ball aflame in the sky and then a beautiful white light. She and Alicia were bathed in this glistening light, and she could feel a presence holding her firmly in the saddle.

Carlin's entire demeanor changed after this experience. She became gracious and much softer. Full of gratitude, she let go of her anger. Carlin had been pushed into the eternal zone beyond our human control. And in that dramatic moment of confrontation, she had surrendered to both the horse and the Divine.

Carlin emerged from this experience profoundly changed. She stopped hanging out on the streets and getting into trouble. She became responsible and less self-centered. Eventually, she left our program and we lost track of her, but she remained in our minds. Then, two years later, while browsing in a large bookstore, we heard someone call our names. We were not close to home and did not expect to meet anyone we knew. Of course, the young woman who came around the side of the shelves to greet us was Carlin, looking very happy and seemingly standing in light. She was ecstatic to see us, and told us of her acceptance to a seminary school in another state. She was leaving the next day. We hugged, cried, and exchanged phone numbers.

Carlin was definitely on her way, entering a vocation where she would help others. She also told us that her experience with Alicia that day, bathed in light, had changed her whole being, and that she knew it was some kind of calling. Carlin was going to use what she had learned to help other inner-city kids. She was so grateful and happy.... *Thank you, Alicia!*

THE IMPORTANCE OF OUR CONNECTION TO NATURE

As horse breeders, we continually find parallels between the mystic and the master equestrian. Each new reminder of this affirms what we have learned from the Celtic spiritual traditions. For example, we no longer base our sense of success with a horse on how we feel in the moment. Life has shown us that it is often the most frustrating times, or the times we are at a stalemate, when we are on the threshold of making real progress. Therefore, we train ourselves to maintain our emotional equilibrium even while undergoing an ordeal. We do not presume that our perceptions in the moment tell the whole story; the greatest mysteries often reveal themselves beyond our limited viewpoints.

Similarly, when we feel disconnected from the spiritual world, we can turn to horses, just as we turned to the land, to bring this awareness back to our consciousness. If we learn to listen, with patience and reverence, the earth and all its creatures can motivate us to reconnect with our innate wisdom, the part that is most attuned to the rhythms of life. When we become discouraged with our own progress, horses urge us to keep going, to pursue the inner path that connects us with Oneness.

The equestrian on a mystical path trains herself to be horse-centered instead of self-centered. In the process, she is reshaped by growing perceptions of a truth much larger than her separate Ego, and larger than the activities shared with the horse. The farmer who lives close to the land, learning to hear its messages, knows that he is not alone but that he works with a much larger entity, with its own rhythms and seasons. Having fully recognized this, he becomes a philosopher of life, not merely a laborer. Farmer and philosopher alike must have vision, which demands an intense involvement with the present, a remembrance of the past, and a dedication to the future.

The more we divorce ourselves from the land and the animals, the more separated from ourselves and the basic truths of our lives we become. It is impossible to deny the correlation, in our modern world, between how increasingly out of touch we are from our food sources and our ability to ignore and even abuse the health of the planet that supports us. Not only does it lead to personal and environmental health problems, it may well be the cause of much societal dysfunction. And when we also become disconnected from our ancestors, and lose all perspective on our responsibility to the future, we lose touch with age-old wisdom, with the lessons drawn from a close connection with nature. Many Native Americans, as well as other indigenous peoples the world over, speak of all life on earth as being part of a continuum, connecting us with both the ancient ones from the past and the ones not yet born. Nowhere is this lesson more clear than in the agrarian community where our actions today, often based on what we have learned from the past, impact our futures, be it the next harvest of grapes or our relationship with a horse.

The Marvels of Staying Rooted

Rather than dwelling on the tragedies of history or of our own lives, it is much more beneficial to remember the brightest lessons from our past, the ancient wisdom and traditions. The world's wisdom community — the repository of universal, beneficial knowledge — shapes our inner core because it teaches us how to see beyond our personal limits. When this happens, life sparkles. By contrast, social conditioning to the fleeting fancies of contemporary life disconnects us from the continuum, making us and the world around us dull; our behavior becomes rote, we act unconsciously, and we are no longer responsive to the now.

The following story gives us a sense of the potency of a wisdom community, of how it provides a special rootedness that supports us and allows us to thrive even when we are otherwise uprooted and disconnected.

Ali was from Jordan, and he had achieved much success in international finance. He came to visit us because he longed to reunite with horses; he had received so much from them in his early life. For generations he and his family had raised Arabian horses in Jordan, and they were steeped in the ancient horse-breeding tradition of the Middle East. His father was an ambassador and also the sheik of his tribe. Since they were of such high standing, the family kept their horses at the king's stable.

Ali explained that he had spent the last year in the United States on extended business, and he was homesick for his horses. In visiting many Arabian ranches in the States, he felt disillusioned because they had not retained the classic standard, nor had they preserved the sweet temperament that the Arabian horses of the Middle East have.

We told Ali that the Peruvian horses we bred were very different than the Arabians he was used to. He said this was something he already knew, but that he had heard about the quality of our horses through the grapevine, and he really wanted to tour our ranch.

Feeling flattered and knowing what a fantastic horseman he must be, we asked him if he wanted to try a horse. He was enthusiastic to do so, and we put him on one of our fiery mares, Estrella, knowing he would enjoy a challenge.

As soon as he sat in the saddle, he made an impression on his mare. Estrella instantly sensed the knowledge of many generations of horse-lovers, equestrians, and breeders flowing through Ali's veins. Within moments, Estrella was at his service, willing, ready, and awaiting his command. Ali had completely captivated her by his very presence.

He asked us, humbly, if he should ride in any particular style. We instructed him to ride just as he would in Jordan, knowing he had already established a powerful relationship with his mare. He positioned himself slightly forward, and within ten minutes, they flew like the wind. As we watched, it seemed we were instantly transported to the Middle East. And so, clearly, was the horse. When Ali transmitted his culture to her, Estrella no longer looked like a Peruvian; before our eyes she physically transformed into an Arabian horse. This in itself was spine-tingling. An Arabian horse's conformation — that is, its body type, its way of moving, and its temperament — is vastly different than a Peruvian's. Arabians are desert horses with high-set tails and a dish face. They have a beautiful dwell, or pause, in their gait.

We could see that, as a result of his profound love for his culture and his years of submersion in a horse tradition, Ali literally embodied this wisdom, perhaps in every cell of his being. He could easily communicate this vision to the horse without even thinking about it. We marveled at his ability. Ali never used legs, stirrups, or reins.

Ali's ride was a living example of how powerful and effective one's roots and history can be. It also illustrated for us the vast difference between the Middle East horse culture he embodied and our modern, industrial culture in our relations to nature and animals. Instead of bringing love, beauty, and *rootedness,* as Ali did, we bring insatiable and irreverent acquisitiveness, the dark traits of a culture barely weathering the onslaught of consumerism. People don't care what their forefathers and mothers did. As a result, few know or have any conception of what actually happens on farms, how to care for animals, or even how to hear the quiet mysticism that informs us when we stop to truly listen.

Most people in modern times rarely witness the farmer working around the clock; they don't realize the time and energy that go into running a horse operation. Too often, the way horse facilities around the United States are run exemplifies how estranged we have become from nature, and from the animals who would be our teachers. As people arrive, the animals are groomed, saddled, and ready to ride. This is most convenient for the equestrian, but it creates a distorted vision, creating a relationship with the animal that is no more intimate or illuminating than getting behind the wheel of an automobile. It is in the caring that we learn; it is in the day-to-day struggles and joys, as we witness the mingling of the mundane and the Divine, that we connect with our Source. It is here we discover the mystical bonds with ancient, timeless wisdom. Truly, the parable of living close to the vine holds an immutable truth that should be an inspiration and a warning for us all.

CHAPTER 8

Dropping Our Illusions

To advance their self-knowledge, Celtic people went to spiritual directors for counsel — both human and animal. They wanted feedback not just from humans but from sources closer to the cosmic realm, and horses willingly provide this.

As one becomes more deeply involved with horses, one begins to have the vague sense that there's another level of communication, another reality just barely beyond our reach. We try, but we are not quite sure how to extend our reach just that little bit more. This is where the journey into the mystical realm with horses truly begins.

Ironically, the first clue that we've stepped onto this mystical path is a feeling that we're at a dead end, or even that we're disconnected from the horse — at least as we've related to it so far. It's important to recognize this clue and not misread it; we need to accept the disconnection we're feeling and remain patient, knowing it is not exactly what it seems to be. As we do this, the transformation of our relationship with the horse, and within ourselves, begins. It soon becomes clear that we must sacrifice our more immediate, Ego-centered goals in order to make room for something much bigger and more promising — the mystical.

Julie, a client who worked with us some years ago, offers an intriguing illustration of how this transformation can occur. Growing up, Julie hadn't been exposed to art or culture. She had never visited art exhibits or museums, developed an ear for music, or attended theater or dance performances. Her early life had been austere and lacked an appreciation of beauty, to put it mildly.

After high school, Julie left home vowing never to return. She was determined to start a new life, and she did. She went to college, and then became a successful financial advisor. However, when the time came for her to be promoted and move up the corporate ladder, something always seemed to interfere with her advancement. She was passed up for promotions time and time again. Objectively, she knew she was qualified to advance in her job, but something was missing, and she didn't know what.

Julie came to us wanting to learn to ride a horse. It was time, she said, to fulfill her childhood dream. To us, Julie appeared well-rounded in her life, for she had learned to compensate well for the deprivations of her upbringing. In fact, we never would have guessed any of it until Julie sat atop a horse. But once she started riding, despite her good intentions and love for the animals, she could not connect. On the back of a horse, Julie looked like a vulture. Every mannerism and move she made called attention to a lack of grace and polish. Fortunately, Julie was not a quitter. She was determined to ride well.

We decided to see what would happen if she stopped riding and worked with horses on the ground. We wanted her to learn to dance with her equine partner. We taught her basic dance steps and had her listen to all kinds of music. We also encouraged her to take painting classes in order to develop her eye for beauty. In the weeks ahead, Julie handled the horses faithfully and refrained from riding. In time she gained more finesse with them on the ground. She learned grace of movement as she danced with them.

Months passed, and Julie got the urge to ride again. When she announced this to us, we were delighted. This time when she mounted, she and the horse were transformed, both equally poised and moving beautifully together. It was quite evident that something important had occurred during the time Julie had taken to develop a sense of beauty and to make her own inner refinement a priority. Not only had she developed her sense of grace, she had also learned to ride by osmosis: that is, by watching others as she worked with the horses on the ground.

Julie no longer felt desolate, and the horses responded to her changes almost instantly. But they were not the only ones who recognized her changes. She had accepted the invitation to attend God's lavish banquet, and now she was ready to receive what perhaps had previously seemed beyond her reach. Shortly after she started riding horses successfully, she was given a promotion in her work. She had transformed her mode of thought from scarcity to abundance, and this changed her external life. From that point forward, she exuded a sense of poise and grace in all her activities.

More often than not, when we examine ourselves carefully, we discover that when we experience obstacles to creativity and prosperity, our Egos are to blame. Often we spend a great deal of our lives painstakingly protecting ourselves and developing our egos into Egos, only to receive exactly what we have been guarding against. For example, we may worry that supplies are limited and fear we may not survive. Our very desperation and anxiety blocks us from creating or experiencing abundance, and so, no matter what happens, it never seems enough and all we continue to know is scarcity. Or, we believe that in order to get ahead we need to fight over even the most meager scraps that are thrown to us, scrounging for whatever comes our way. We want to pursue our dreams, but we feel compelled to always grab what's easily within reach, and so we keep closing the door to what our hearts truly desire. All these reactions are Ego driven.

On a horse, the human Ego often indulges the fantasy that we will excel immediately, advancing and reaping great rewards without sacrifice and without suffering any hardships. The hallmark of an unbalanced Ego is its relentless desire for instant gratification. Despite how smoothly our Ego thinks things should go, when it comes to horses, it usually doesn't work that way. The horse will not be bullied into doing what we want, except, perhaps, when performing the most menial chores. In fact, our illusions of grandeur, of becoming an instant equestrian, are often frustrated. Harmony can be reached with a horse only by cultivating a spirit of giving and generosity that mirrors the horse's own.

Being deeply rooted in eternal values, horses always side with the soul; they push us to aspire toward what is lasting and real, so that we can eventually experience nature's true bounty. Julie, for example, learned that she had to drop her Ego-driven need to advance in order to become competent on horseback. She chose a humble approach, which is always the best path, by developing her relationship with the horse on the ground and preparing her own interior for the job that lay ahead. It could be said that Julie learned to ride only when she agreed to stand beside her horse, not sit on top of it.

If we ever hope to progress from ordinary to extraordinary

in any of our endeavors — be it horseback riding, cooking, art, dance, music, or business — we must tame our Egos. We need to willfully sacrifice our own self-centered concerns and preoccupations so that spirit can flow through us. This is at the heart of the mystical way; it is the stage of spiritual development when we are challenged to follow divine will, to serve spirit instead of ourselves.

This mystical zone of spiritual development is taxing to our psyches. It takes psychic stamina to voluntarily place ourselves in a position of vulnerability and to allow ourselves to risk failure. As adults, we work hard to gain a reasonable amount of worldly know-how and success, and the mystical path leads us to confront those deeply buried human fears of incompetence, insignificance, and meaninglessness. Upon revisiting these existential fears, where we cannot escape feelings of uncertainty and discomfort, we are forced to find new paths of meaning. In time we discover that this humbling state is the only place where we can reconnect with the ground of our being, the fertile ground of new creation and passion.

If we can learn to accept this disconcerting state, in which our self-importance significantly diminishes, we will find the spiritual path and its incomparable rewards. The horse is a great teacher, encouraging us to acknowledge our vulnerability and human limitations and to renew our ties with the community of creatures. Although we relinquish our feelings of superiority, we are paradoxically infused with a new kind of potency as we reconnect to the Divine. Our potential becomes limitless.

Through acts of communion in this state of vulnerability, fostered through our connections with earth's creatures, we place ourselves under God's care and free ourselves from whatever human brokenness has created the barrier that is stopping us. This is the sure way to increase the quality of our lives and set free our inner being. By placing our trust in a higher power rather than seeing ourselves as the only source, doors open to us in a way they never could on our own. By surrendering in this way, we enter a state of unceasing prayer, as advocated by the Celts. This state of prayer becomes no longer something we do, but a way of being.

Maintaining the Mystical Connection in Competition

Surges of passion and love urge us forward on this challenging mystical path; these arise from our inner depths, emanating as if from a simmering and unspoken romance. On the mystical path, we enter into a direct relationship with God. The mystery of this relationship unfolds as we get glimmers of the cosmic design and the magnitude of the love that's available to us. We return to simplicity, perceiving how little we need beyond the quest itself, the search for the Divine within ourselves, within the horse, and within the connection developing between the two of us.

For people who are already involved in the equestrian community — where competition at horse shows often takes center stage — the mystical path can pose many new challenges. From the mystical vantage point, it's clear that horses suffer when they are exploited for the purpose of aggrandizing their riders or owners. But participation in horse shows doesn't need to turn into an egotistical contest. When we honor the mystical path, we infuse every activity with a spiritual undercurrent. We can bring a different set of values to events and competitions by setting different standards for our own behavior, by maintaining our mystical connection with our horses regardless of the activity we're engaged in. Competitions themselves don't necessarily interfere with the mystical path, but the way we participate in them can.

The more casual, recreational rider should first learn to ride for passion, not competition, and in our horse programs we design special activities to foster this. At our new ranch just outside San Antonio, Texas, we bring the caves of Granada, Spain, to us. We have fiestas, with flamenco dancers and guitarists. While mounted, we allow the horses to dance along, following the flamenco troupe and the driving rhythm of the castanets. The horses thrive on these rhythms because their natural Peruvian Paso gait of "one, two, three, four" is a flamenco beat.

Any sense of competition dissolves into enthusiasm and passion as we reconnect with the wild nature of the dance. We use flamenco because it is a dance of raw passion and divine inspiration. As the gypsies in Spain say, we get closer to the flame of life in the dance of flamenco because we drink from Christ's cup of blood. On horseback, for both horse and rider, it is similar to the dance of the whirling dervish.

Living Daily in the Center Point

The hallmark of the mystic equestrian is to live in the center point, which is frequently symbolized in ancient traditions by the flame. Symbolically, the mystic equestrian lives closer to the fire; our lives become more heated, alive, and intense, yet we find we can handle the additional heat without much anxiety. In the center of the flame, our false self, or public identity, is diminished, while at the same time we become more effective and more deeply satisfied in our lives. As challenging as this might sound, if we fail to venture into this region of fire, or fail to confront our own "graven image," we can never cultivate our creativity and spiritual development to their maximum.

We locate this region of creativity and mysticism through ancient prayer practices, engaging in the artistry of horsemanship and a process of impeccable reflection. We observe how we act with our equine companions and take note of our own behavior, feelings, and attitudes without analyzing or criticizing them. We explore and discover what is inside of us that interferes with the horse reaching its potential.

When we observe our interactions in this way, we learn three important lessons: First, we learn who we are, not who we *think* we are. Second, we discover what we might be doing that limits or hinders our interactions. Third, we see alternate courses we might take to improve the way we relate to the world. What better way to learn about our own inner nature than through the reactions of a horse?

Jessica, a project manager at a large company, learned about leadership while on one of our equine retreats. At work, her team repeatedly failed to complete their assignments, but Jessica did not connect this low productivity to her own leadership style. She instead thought of herself as a dynamic leader, and her favorite metaphors evoked the military; she spoke about her employees as if they were her troops and she their general.

And yet, Jessica shared countless examples of how her staff ignored her, as if they had forgotten that she was the team leader. Those who worked under Jessica treated her like an invisible woman. Jessica was blind to the fact that her staff did not see her as their general at all — and had actually staged something of a coup to depose her — and she lacked insight into the part she was playing to create this situation.

Jessica was working the horse on the ground on a long rope called a longe line. This way of working not only exercises and trains the horse for the maneuvers and gaits it will do under saddle; it tests a person's communication with the horse. It can show a breakdown in communication: if a horse is asked by a handler to walk and all it does is run, for example.

Jessica finally woke up when Magna, our filly, not only ran wildly on the longe line but made threatening moves toward her. The horse not only refused to listen to Jessica's request to walk but flatly and aggressively rebelled. Jessica quickly discovered that acting like a five-star general and shouting orders didn't work with Magna. Magna challenged her authority time and time again. In fact, Jessica's repertoire of "leadership skills" only made Magna angrier and more rebellious. Magna knew Jessica was playing a role, and she was not willing to play that game. As her false self crumbled, Jessica began to cry. At last, she became real and able to let her authentic self emerge.

Confronted with this realization, and the need to change, Jessica spent the week undoing all the leadership techniques she had been employing. She abandoned rhetoric such as "deploying forces." As Jessica's relationship with Magna improved, she discovered she did not have to be militant to be a leader. In fact, she learned that she had inner resources that produced much better results. With inner conviction and a more realistic sense of self, she was able to verbally and non-verbally make deeper connections with her horse and work with her more amicably. After experiencing these changes in her relationship with Magna, Jessica returned to work and found she was finally able to gain the respect and cooperation of her coworkers.

While approaching horses in these ways may seem mystical, it is never lofty. First, we must begin from the assumption that until we are united with a force greater than ourselves (call it God or whatever you will), our human nature is limited. As a rider, we shift our focus so that we acknowledge our own part in the process, rather than standing outside the action and trying only to change or control the horse. We are thus challenged to amend our own attitudes, perceptions, behaviors, priorities, and reactions when they get in the way. We help the horse by gaining self-control and awareness. We learn to start from the premise that reality (in this case, the horse) is fine; if there is a problem, we need to look at our perception of that reality. To enter into the whole that is our relationship with the horse, we must change our perception and act differently until we find the approach that brings harmony. This is the essence of the self-awakening process; it is one of peeling away the layers of the false self until only the real self remains. Only then can we recognize our original nature. Through deliberate contemplation we extract the toxins and unearth the gold buried in ourselves and in Creation.

SPIRITUAL DIRECTION, THE CELTIC WAY

The basis of Celtic spiritual direction is, first and foremost, to drop our false self and become real. Spirituality without this is futile. It leads to illusion. To that end, the Celts grounded and conducted their psychospiritual analysis in the heart of nature. This kept interactions with one another, nature, and their horses real and robust.

Animals play a key role in keeping our intentions honest. Since they cannot be swayed or charmed by what the Spanish call our *palabra* — or our false illusions about ourselves — they force us to develop more honest and direct avenues of communication, a heart-to-heart connectedness. The Celts were wise in knowing that too much analysis and exegesis (exploration or interpretation of the Scriptures) is another form of intellectual self-absorption that separates us from our true selves. Anytime we get caught up in pursuing what is trendy and popular, it is usually our Egos that are driving us. The Celtic mystics — along with mystics of other traditions, such as the Sufis and many Native American peoples — rightly suggested that too much talk about anything leads us into egocentricity.

Focusing on nature is an invaluable component of any spiritual growth program. Any method, regardless of how valuable it may seem, will fail if the quest to understand our relationship to nature is missing. When removed and distanced from the forces of nature, we tend to go off on tangents, creating whole worlds in our heads. For example, in both Jungian and Freudian analysis, it is possible to become so self-involved delving into dreams or sexual problems that the delving itself becomes more important than the outcome those methods were intended to produce. Being rooted in nature prevents this kind of imbalance because it reminds us of what is valuable so that we do not get lost, or stuck, in life's minutiae.

To advance their self-knowledge, Celtic people went to spiritual directors for counsel — both human and animal. They wanted feedback not just from humans but from sources closer to the cosmic realm, and horses willingly provide this. Indeed, in reviewing early Celtic literature, we discovered that Pelagius, the fourth-century Celtic theologian, approached his directees in the same way that our horses approach people today. In Pelagius's letters to various directees, he encourages them to find their own answers by looking deeply into their own hearts and examining their own consciences. When they do, he explains, they will begin to discover a real self that is connected to the Divine. Pelagius challenged people to exercise their will, learn from their mistakes, and develop inner strengths. Although Pelagius believed in grace, he strongly advocated personal empowerment. He wanted his students to take responsibility for their own inner development and life choices. Both Pelagius and our horses share an aversion to the false self.

An excellent example with our horses comes from one of our equine retreats with Betty, a successful school administrator. When she arrived, she acted extremely depressed. She lacked confidence and energy. She shuffled around. She was forty-nine but behaved like seventy, and not a very healthy seventy at that. Her voice quivered and crackled, and she looked as if she were carrying the weight of the world on her shoulders. Her whole demeanor suggested she had not only given up on herself and life but wanted others to feel sorry for her. She embodied the adage "Misery loves company."

Betty loved horses but could never manage to connect with them in the way that she felt must be possible. She was overly affectionate and doted on them. She tried to bribe them by giving them too many carrots and apples. Her idea of getting close was to hang onto the animal and pet it to death. She didn't realize that horses hate being smothered. Horses are more like human teenagers, who want a healthy distance from their parents.

Betty came to the retreat because our book *Horse Sense and the Human Heart* had sparked her interest. After reading it, she had been excited, something she had not felt in years. Yet her excitement was short-lived. Once she was introduced to the horses, she deflated. Once her dream was no longer a fantasy, her feelings of fear and inadequacy resurfaced.

We brought out Manuel, one of our sweetest geldings. Betty was nervous but learned the basics of lunging and riding on the first day, since prior to coming she had been taking riding lessons. Nonetheless, she could not get the horse to go straight or turn right or left. In the saddle, she was hunched over, and her whole body was limp. Betty lacked spine and will. She lacked any center, physical, mental, or spiritual. She understood spiritual concepts inside-out but had not yet applied them in her daily life. In a very real way, her spirituality was compartmentalized, something that was totally in her head and held by her Ego.

Betty was scared while riding, and she knew it. In the course of working with us, she told the story of her experiences with a previous riding instructor. When she told him that she was afraid of horses, he told her she was "silly." After seeing her lack of balance and communication with Manuel, we assured

Betty that she was fully justified in her fear. She *should* have been scared, since she lacked some fundamental skills and was simply at the mercy of the horse!

On the second day, we decided Betty should work with Manuel while on the ground. We wanted her to establish some communication and develop some *oomph* before we put her back on a horse. If she couldn't make an impact on the ground, there was no reason to sit her on a horse. People don't realize that it is far easier to get a horse's attention on the ground than it is when you are in the saddle.

Even on the ground, Manuel had Betty's number. He made two full circles of the arena, plodding along like a turtle. He knew he was on his own. Betty gave him no direction, no commands, and no emotional support. So he simply pulled on the rope, dragged her a few feet, and began to eat. Betty's solution was to simply give him the lead and follow along. She acted completely helpless and powerless.

Even watching from afar, we could see Betty beginning to steam. Beneath her frail and wilted exterior, she was fuming. It was the first sign of life any of us had seen. Betty was furious at Manuel for not listening to her. In no time, she discovered that Manuel was better than she was at her game of being passive-aggressive and obstinate. He was giving Betty a dose of her own medicine, and she didn't like it. He refused to do anything. Then he furiously shook his head at her and pinned back his ears. In horse language, he was swearing at her. Betty stepped back a few feet. As she put this distance between herself and Manuel, she realized she had taken this horse for granted.

Betty had completely misread Manuel. Because he was sweet, she had treated him like a useless object. As a result, he was angry. She had never considered that there might be another side to his personality, so she had never tried to bring it out.

In Peru they call Manuel's kind of spirit *brio escondido.* This means that the horse has spirit, but it is hidden. Only the rider who puts his own heart, soul, and energy into such a horse, and challenges it to be more than what it is presenting, can bring this hidden spirit to the surface. This requires the efforts of a rider who loves all horses, not just the easy ones.

Betty soon realized there was nothing wrong with Manuel... except that he was bored with her. When others picked up his rope, Manuel would collect himself and get excited. However, when it was Betty's turn, he would only saunter.

Initially, Betty used this awareness to feel sorry for herself. Then we asked her to reverse roles and put herself in the horse's place. When she did that, she was stunned to see how lifeless she was being. Betty had become a shell.

Instead of remaining angry and perturbed with the horse, she began to empathize with him. What a job this horse had! Manuel had aroused Betty's anger so that she might finally use it for good instead of always turning it inward upon herself. She began to belly-laugh, thinking about Manuel. She had never met a horse with his mettle. Even as Manuel was waiting for Betty to take charge, Betty was expecting Manuel to take care of her. What a pair! Betty soon learned that a relationship with a horse must be collaborative, with horse and person each giving equally to the relationship. The time had come for her to do her part.

Betty now had to literally and figuratively carry her own weight. Manuel was not about to give an inch if she didn't motivate herself. Betty had played helpless and weak for years, getting her way by making others feel sorry for her. Now Manuel demanded that if Betty genuinely loved horses, she would have to give up her passivity with them. He wanted her to act like a horsewoman and rise to the challenge. The challenge was to dig for her hidden strengths, talents, and passions, which she had buried. The horse knew that Betty had value, and he wanted her to find it. Manuel challenged Betty to get rid of her false self, the helpless and weak persona that impeded her progress.

By the fifth day Betty was on her way to becoming a rider instead of a whiner. We were overjoyed. She sat up tall in the saddle, thinking clearly, smiling, and taking charge. She even refused to buckle when Manuel resisted turning. At last Betty looked like an equestrian! She and Manuel glided around the arena like a team. They did beautiful figure eights, serpentines, and stops. Betty was flying high, and so was the horse. Betty had overcome her continuing bouts of fear by using the meditative prayer we had given her on horseback. It helped her regain her cool.

At the end of the retreat, it was obvious that Manuel loved Betty, and Betty loved him. Each partner had grown closer as they challenged each other to dig deeper and find their essential goodness, strength, and beauty, affirming their connection with God. Manuel knew there was more to Betty, and Betty, likewise, discovered how much inner depth and wisdom resided in her new equine friend.

Betty left the retreat a new person. Her equine experience had been life-changing. She returned home enthusiastic about life, instead of feeling downtrodden and demoralized. Her energy came back, and her burnout was gone. Her life at work and home became more joyful. She was no longer a pushover, but had found the balance between healthy aggression and love. Manuel had helped Betty regain something she'd lost, her divine identity.

The Celtic way always challenges people and animals to reach deeper inside and find the riches buried there. It also requires people to assume responsibility for their lives. When people dig for their inner resources, instead of collapsing into weakness or disability, they find God at the center. In that process, they transcend their own limitations because they find God within themselves. When this happens, the horse responds positively to them, and as their inner awareness expands, horse and rider become players in the unfolding drama of the soul.

THEATER OF THE INVISIBLE

Once someone has experienced the mystical realm, whether through his or her work with horses or some other practice, the person soon realizes the material plane is not the main show but only a piece of a much larger, unseen drama. It is here, in this unseen realm, that we can create breakthroughs that truly alter our lives forever. When we learn to stretch and expand our consciousness, such as in the ways explored in this book, we begin to recognize that there are two planes of reality from which we can draw. Some refer to these planes as the temporal and the eternal. Others describe them as the mundane and the cosmic. Still others refer to them as the literal and the symbolic. Whatever these planes are called, as you become immersed in the mystical you begin to see, in all your endeavors, not just one but at least two coexisting realities — that which we perceive with our five senses and one that we perceive with our hearts and our souls.

We find another view of this same idea illuminated in one of the earliest Vedic mystical texts. The Vedic seer reaches an understanding of the threefold nature of the world, at once physical, psychological, and spiritual. These three worlds are inseparable, every physical reality having psychological and spiritual aspects, and vice versa. In the Vedas, cows and horses are not merely cows and horses — they are also cows and horses of the mind, or psychological forces, and beyond that they are symbols of the cosmic powers, manifestations of the Supreme Spirit.[1]

In Western culture, the symbolism of the Celtic cross — a cross within a circle — reflects archetypes concerning the threefold nature of the universe, as well as the ensuing cyclical processes that are inherent in the natural order of the Cosmos. The intersecting vertical and horizontal planes of the cross represent ways the invisible world is continually impacting our own lives. The circle represents the regenerative and creative forces that are at work in all of life, forces that are eternal, natural, and cyclical. What begins ends and begins and ends again. Even the cyclical turns out to be an aspect of the eternal.

Those who pursue the mystical path with horses don't necessarily seek otherworldly experiences. Nevertheless, they do occur, sometimes spontaneously. The process usually begins with seeing everyday experiences in a new light, and then acknowledging the mystery that lies at the heart of the mundane and the ordinary. We learn to recognize the existence of the mystical forces inside and outside us, and then learn to follow their direction, rather than trying to introduce something new or force a change upon ourselves.

Living the way of the cross and circle can become so compelling that it radically transforms every facet of our being. This vision of life shatters past illusions of reality, and we can no longer live with the superficial perceptions that once gave us comfort. We thirst to return to what is most essential in the world, in ourselves, and in one another, and we begin to drink each day from those living waters.

Through direct and personal encounters with the Divine, with the horse as our messenger, we begin to grasp that making and sustaining a relationship with the One is not just incidental to our well-being or creativity but is essential. It is necessary to our ongoing human health and happiness, for we learn that this is the most natural place to be.

CONSECRATED WORK

We enter this other reality through the wisdom and intelligence of our hearts. In the process we abandon all sentimentality. For the passion of horse-human interactions to transform into mystical insight and revelation, the quality of our love needs to ripen and mature. This is an important aspect of spiritual cross-training. We learn that on the spiritual road, the bounty we eventually receive is never self-generated as much as it is an act of grace. In that respect, the goodness arising from our relationship with horses can be viewed as God-given, not something we willfully and self-consciously create. We can no longer claim to be sole creators of our life experience but must view ourselves as cocreators, becoming open and responsive collaborators with the invisible reality that we may enter with the horse.

As this experience of grace unfolds in our lives, harmony more than technique becomes our focal point. If there is a self-conscious aspect of the experience, it is in our discovery of what we must do to nurture our relationships so that this certain kind of interaction can occur. We learn what kinds of atmospheres and attitudes foster harmonious action and responsiveness. As a sacred phenomenon, the horse experience is consecrated by devotion, immersion, humility, and commitment. Here, touching the center of our being, we connect with the tempestuous and exhilarating terrain of the religious, where spirit emerges.

CHAPTER 9

The Spiritual Instinct

Horses have fulfilled their Celtic legacy by awakening the spiritual instinct in all of us. Since the beginning, they have served us, and the people who've worked with us, as messengers, angels, guides, matchmakers, merrymakers, and vigil holders. In very subtle ways they have always been there to push us in the right direction, particularly when we took the time to listen to and heed their clues.

Although the ancient Celts were tribal, anyone who embraced their wisdom, ideals, and virtues, including any of the world's creatures, was adopted as a "kinsman." During their travels the Celts not only influenced other cultures but were influenced by them. Since they loved and easily incorporated the customs of many peoples, they tended to be what in family systems theory we'd call an open system. Open systems are healthy, fostering attitudes of acceptance and respect for each person's individuality. One might even say that being a Celt was, and is, a state of mind rather than a national or religious affiliation. Whoever has an affinity toward the Celtic Way is indeed a Celt.

It is only in recent times that the Celts have been defined as people from Ireland, Scotland, and Wales. Perhaps a better way to understand the Celtic Way is that it opens doors to a timeless, nonlocal brotherhood, one that offers an expansive way of being in the world, embracing people from all religions and cultural backgrounds.

Whatever one's ethnicity or spiritual understanding, be it Christianity, Buddhism, Islam, Judaism, or the way of the Creative Goddess, we all interact with the forces and furies of the Cosmos. On both real and metaphorical levels, these are embodied in the horse. Central to Celtic teachings, the lessons horses offer can help us learn to live joyfully in a state somewhere between knowing and not-knowing, between wisdom and innocence. The mind that emerges from this way of life is flexible and open, holding the wisdom that to be free we must learn to tolerate contradictions and look beyond our prejudices. We call this unique state of mind a *religious mind.*

Developing a religious mind is central to our interior growth. It involves filling ourselves with God's spirit. Instead of living in a directionless and haphazard way, the mind needs to be trained to be still, uncluttered, and centered. In that respect, the horse's lessons are quite demanding and precise; to be truly present and connect with the horse, we must immerse ourselves in the moment. We do this by educating our minds to stay on target, and liberating ourselves from fixations on past trauma or perceived injustices.

By engaging in this kind of inner work, we find the extraordinary in the ordinary world. As we gain increasing mental discipline and harmony in our relationship with horses, we begin to discern the unseen dimension of spirit that coexists with our material reality. In turn, we cultivate what can only be called a religious or spiritual instinct, a deep desire to be with God, which activates our souls.

Except for Carl Jung, few psychologists have fully explored this instinct. In his book *On Psychic Energy,* Jung asserted: "The spiritual appears in the psyche as an instinct, indeed a real *passion*.... It is not derived from any other instinct, but is a principle *sui generic,* that is, a specific and necessary form of instinctual power."[1]

Similarly, the famous artist Matisse spoke about his own innate sense of God: "Do I believe in God? Yes I do, when I am working. When I am submissive and modest, I feel surrounded by someone who makes me do things of which I am not capable."[2] It was through his work that Matisse felt this extraordinary connection with the mystery, and with God, a connection that was direct and immediate, not filtered through the hierarchy of an organized religion or any other human paradigm. What our work with horses has confirmed for us, many times over, is that when we are able to embrace this instinctual power of the spirit, and allow it to guide us in a way very much like Matisse describes, we find a sanctuary or spiritual nourishment, fortification, and hospitality.

One must dig very deep to find wisdom teachings such as these in any of today's religious organizations. The center of Celtic teachings is mystical. However, delving into the world of mystery was removed from the Western Judeo-Christian tradition around 400 A.D. by St. Augustine of Hippo, who branded Pelagius, a Celtic theologian, a heretic for his progressive ideas and mystical views. Mysticism was officially forbidden by the church during the Reformation, which began with Martin Luther, around 1517 A.D. Thereafter any inner knowledge was labeled heretical, the focus on sin was intensified, and a sense of the mystery was lost. After the Reformation religion became exoteric, not esoteric. It also became dualistic, robbing the world of its sanctity.

The mystical path fosters inner empowerment and liberation

while putting the individual in direct contact with God. It teaches us skills for becoming strong, independent, and courageous human beings. In our own lives, during the time when we were unable to find that kind of direction in modern religion, we were able to find it with the aid of our horses and the lessons outlined in the ancient Celtic traditions. The mystical path is not a "feel-good" type of spirituality, although it can certainly lead to a profound sense of inner peace, unparalleled satisfaction, and joy. The mystical path virtually demands that we learn to relinquish our small egotistical self. In its place we learn to take in the wisdom and power of the Source, stretching our minds and hearts to gain lasting and intangible delight.

Religion, in the sense we use in this book, refers to a spiritual process that requires us to go deeper and resurface with a new image of ourselves and our relationship to the world.

The actual word *religion*, from the Latin *sacer* and *facere*, means "to make holy or sacred," to sacrifice to a higher purpose, or Source. According to Joseph Shipley, "Since that which is made holy is given over to the Gods, from the human point of view it is given up; hence the meaning of yielding one thing to gain another."[3] By yielding or sacrificing in this way, we unite our finite human resources with the limitless resources available in Creation and implanted in the depths of our soul. Through our ever-increasing understanding of unchangeable and eternal truths, we break free; we become more fully ourselves by accessing the Divine in ourselves and others, and so begin to love expansively in each moment.

The Mystical in Everyday Life

You may recall that in chapter 4 we promised to tell you how our stallion, Trianero, came into our lives. Since that story dramatically illustrates the power of the spiritual instinct in everyday life, it seems most relevant to share that story here. It began with our desire to bring Peruvian horses into our work. The more we learned about this breed, the more we believed that, with their excellent minds and strong hearts, they would make a major contribution with our clients. We decided to start with a few mares. With that in mind, we set out to visit a horse show where we could meet with top breeders and see some of their horses in competition.

It is important to note here that at this time Tom was not actively participating in any sort of spiritual practice or religion. Nevertheless, he believed in God. Like Matisse, his spiritual instinct was expressed in his work.

As we drove home from the horse show, Tom could not stop talking about a particular horse he had seen. He said this was the finest horse he had ever encountered, and it had been a spectacular experience to watch it as it won the championship in its class. We were amazed that even though he'd seen this horse only from afar, he had made such a powerful connection with it. He even knew this horse's Spanish name. Somehow, he had tuned into this horse without any effort whatsoever and now held it close to his heart.

While Tom was making this amazing connection, the rest of us were still trying to orient ourselves to the different classes and horses in the show. We could barely tell one horse from another. Tom recalled that as he watched this horse move around the arena, he spontaneously began to pray. He thanked God for giving him the opportunity to behold such a beautiful creature. Tom didn't ask God for anything; he only expressed gratitude. He felt that a horse of this caliber had been put on the earth just to grace the world with his presence.

Tom knew that this horse would not be for sale. Even if it had been, we would have had little chance of purchasing such a stallion. As it was a champion, the price would have been quite outside our range. But breeders rarely sell horses of this caliber since they are the result of many decades of breeding and are generally kept for show and for breeding. Inexplicably drawn to this horse, Tom felt that merely watching him was a gift and blessing that he would carry with him for the rest of his life. He realized he would be content to one day own an animal that was even half the horse this one was.

A few months after this show, we had a surprise phone call from a man who had had a booth selling saddles and bridles at the show. He had good news for us. Tom had won first prize in a raffle at the booth. The prize was an all-expense-paid trip to the National Horse Show in Lima, Peru, which is the finest horse show in the country. We were elated and delighted to be able to make the trip.

Tom and Adele spent a week in Lima. The horses were dazzling, and the riders were all highly skilled equestrians. It was an extravaganza of horses. Parties were held every evening, with celebrities from all over the world flocking there to join in the festivities. The horses were so loved by their owners that there was a spirit about the whole event that was uplifting and inspiring, unlike any show Tom and Adele had ever attended in the United States. While there, they met many Peruvian breeders and were invited to visit their private haciendas.

Tom and Adele went to visit one breeder in particular, Don Francisco, whose family had bred famous horses for decades in Spain and Peru. Their horses were gorgeous. Watching these animals move was heaven on earth. Meanwhile, their hosts were charming, sharing many things in common with Tom and Adele: life philosophies, spiritual beliefs, views on arts and politics. Don Francisco gave Tom and Adele carte blanche to make themselves completely at home on the ranch.

One morning Adele was out walking when she saw a herd of mares and went into the field to say hello to them. The mares immediately came up to her to visit. After talking with them for a while, Adele was overcome with a sense of joy. It was a warm, sunny day, and she sat down in the meadow to watch her equine friends, feeling completely at home and relaxed. The mares slowly came toward her, and each mare lay down beside her. She was astounded by their trust and love.

That evening, Adele told the story of her experience to her hosts. They were delighted. Don Francisco smiled and said it was a good sign because the mares sensed her friendship and love. As Tom and Adele dined with their newfound Peruvian friends, Don Francisco mentioned that he had just shipped a stallion to the States and wanted to move him to California. He asked if we would be willing to accept him at our ranch. Tom and Adele said yes, they'd be glad to care for the horse, though Don Francisco had told them nothing about the stallion they'd be getting. And, stunned by the offer, they asked nothing further. They felt that probing would have been in bad taste.

Before flying home, Tom and Adele returned to Lima, where they found a shop that had a beautifully painted *santo* of San Miguel, patron saint of horses. Such a piece is a rare find. They immediately bought the *santo* and brought it home with them.

Several weeks after their return, the horse transport company arrived with the stallion Don Francisco had promised to send them. We still didn't know which stallion would arrive, although we knew he would be magnificent, based on this breeder's track record and his love for horses. Our hearts raced with anticipation. Before unloading the horse, the driver walked over and handed Tom the stallion's registration papers. Tom looked down, read them, and gasped. The name on the papers was Trianero! This was the horse Tom had made such a powerful connection with at the horse show months before.

Tom's connection with Trianero was much more than a chance encounter with an extraordinary animal. Their meeting had awakened and confirmed Tom's deepest spiritual instincts, providing a connection with that part of him that recognizes the Divine in other beings and in everyday events. This magnificent stallion was a gift in more ways than one, for on that day our wild adventure with God and horses began. Through that amazing connection between horses and humans, Trianero would, over time, serve to awaken the spiritual instinct in many people with whom we have worked. What follows is the story of one of the most challenging and dramatic of those interactions.

Angels among Us

One evening the mother of one of our longtime students phoned. She had some horrible news to share with us about her daughter, Melissa, and she could barely get the words out. Melissa had been diagnosed with cancer, and doctors had given her only six months to live. They offered Melissa and her mother little or no hope, but said that with treatment her life might be spared, at least for a short time. This strain of cancer was a killer. In fact, if Melissa chose treatment, the kind of chemotherapy she'd receive would be extremely potent, risky, and painful. The treatment itself might kill her before the cancer did. However, the head oncologist said that if she were his child, he would take his chances. Death by chemotherapy was preferable to the agonizing death that lay ahead for Melissa without treatment. Melissa's mother was calling us because she did not know where else to turn.

Adele was devastated. She was hardly able to take in this upsetting news. Melissa was one of our favorite students. The young woman originally came to work with the horses when she was having trouble in school. Melissa had been diagnosed with ADD (attention deficit disorder) at the time, and her parents thought horses might help her focus. They did! Melissa had been involved with the horses for years and was becoming a skilled and conscientious equestrian. Moreover, through the years she and her parents had become our friends.

"I need some magic," Melissa's mother said that evening.

Adele answered, "We don't have any magic, but we have our horses, and we pray." She told Melissa's mother that we would do anything we could to help. We would have to take some time, sleep on it, then call her back in the morning.

Our minds reeled, struggling to accept the fact that Melissa had cancer. We could only imagine what her parents must be feeling. Melissa had always been so healthy. She had just turned sixteen and should have had her whole life ahead of her. She had managed to overcome her learning problems and was gregarious and full of life. She had had no physical symptoms until two weeks prior to the diagnosis, when she had recognized two lumps in her throat. She showed them to her mother and her mother made a doctor's appointment. The family thought she only had a case of swollen glands.

Shaken by the call that evening, we prayed silently and asked for direction from God. We had been going to church and taking communion regularly for about a year. As a result, our view about where to find answers had begun to shift. We were becoming more God-centered. Yet we had no preconceived ideas about what was best for Melissa. This was God's call.

That night Trianero, our wonderful stallion, appeared to Adele in a dream. Adele's dream started with her seeing a lifeless child lying on the ground. The child seemed vulnerable and defenseless. Trianero walked up and nuzzled her. His crested neck was arched, and he gently peered down to see if he could be of any help. Trianero had always rescued children and foals in distress.

Adele remembers vividly that once Trianero approached

the lifeless body, he did very little. He just watched over the girl's body like a patient sentinel. Adele thought it was odd that Trianero's countenance was so peaceful. There was no sense of emergency or panic.

In the dream, all three of us had been looking for Trianero. Now, as we caught sight of him, we joined him at the child's side. We couldn't identify the child, but it was obvious that the stallion was holding vigil. Somehow he conveyed to us that we were to slow down and follow his lead. We stood still. Approaching the place where he was standing, we felt vibrant. We stood like statues in a circle around the child and waited. Something was going on that we didn't understand.

Then Trianero broke the stillness and greeted us in his friendly manner. He seemed completely unruffled and very calm about the child we were all watching. When the silence was broken, Tom asked Trianero how we could help Melissa. His message was as clear as day. He looked up at a hill in the distance and motioned with his head, as horses do, to go there. He was pointing us toward a great high cross looming on a hill across the countryside. The hill with the high cross was surrounded by fields of heather and lavender. Adele remembers that the cross was the centerpiece of the landscape.

Adele awakened from the dream deeply moved and told us what had happened. The three of us knew we needed to call our friend Father George. We did so immediately and asked if he would help, even though the family didn't believe in God. He agreed to talk with Melissa and her parents if her parents would permit it. Her parents were both science professors and outspoken atheists. Melissa had never been raised with any religious background, so the visit from a priest would be foreign to her. However, it didn't matter. Melissa and her parents were grateful that someone cared. They immediately gave their permission and were anxious to meet the priest. They asked if the meeting could take place before Melissa's chemo and radiation treatments, which were to start the following week.

We drove Father George over to Melissa's house. He walked in wearing his Celtic cross and traditional cassock. We introduced him to the family, and when Melissa first saw him, she was spellbound. In fact, she fixated on his cross. She went over to admire it and told him that cross was the most beautiful thing she had ever seen. We all prayed, with which Melissa seemed completely comfortable. At the end of the evening, Father George asked Melissa what she most loved to do. She answered that she loved working with horses. He told her, "You keep working with the horses because they are God's messengers, St. Michael himself."

The following week Melissa began her medical treatments. She went through a series of awful radiation therapy. We helped drive her back and forth. Before her first series of treatments, we gave her some meditation techniques with horses to help take her mind off the pain and nausea she'd be experiencing. She bravely went to one department after the other that first day. At each station we found frightened, lonely, and confused people. Our hearts went out to them. We could smell the burning flesh from the radiation; even to this day the odor lingers. Yet for months we just kept going. The hospital became our home away from home.

Melissa would make progress and then go into a slump. Her hair was falling out, her eyes listless, her face ashen. It was a frightful condition for a sixteen-year-old. We continued our hopes and prayers for her. Then we got a call again from her parents. Melissa had taken a turn for the worse. Her tumors were growing again, and the doctor feared that the cancer had metastasized. We were all feeling demoralized and apprehensive. So the next day we went to see Father George and described what was happening. Although we were unaware of it, we must have sounded very dismal and hopeless.

Out of the blue, Father George looked at us and said, "She is not dead yet. Sometimes God waits until the very last moment to heal someone, to prove he is God and we are not." We were startled. His words were forceful and potent. The voice of truth rang out. He suggested we get together with Melissa and do another healing, except this time in church, at the altar. Being dutiful servants, we again got permission from her parents. We also made sure Melissa was comfortable with this plan. She agreed, sobbing because she could feel one of the tumors closing her throat and air passages.

The next day, we picked Melissa up at her home and drove her to church. This was to be a private healing, so Father George was the only one in the church with us. While he was preparing the consecrated healing oil, we asked Melissa if she wanted to walk the labyrinth that was in the garden of the church. She did, and was struck by how disoriented she felt when she came out. She said it threw her mind off balance. "This is great," we told her. "It means your heart and mind will be open to new possibilities."

When we returned to the church, we showed her around. We explained the significance of the art, the stained glass, and the font, hoping it would help her feel more at home. As we finished this tour and were walking up to the altar rail, a well-dressed couple came in the door. The woman looked radiant, and her eyes sparkled. She had silvery white hair and was wearing a beautiful royal-blue suit. Her husband was also dressed very handsomely. They made a stunning couple, and both had an unusual vibrancy.

Since it was late on a Thursday morning, it was unusual to see strangers in the church. They typically visited on Wednesdays or Sundays, when we had worship. Additionally, this church was very hard to find, small and off the beaten track, not the sort of place strangers would happen upon. Nonetheless, the couple walked in asking for Father George by name. The couple said they had been sent by their own priest from Monterey. They asked if they were interrupting. Father George said no, all were welcome here. He continued, "We are just about to do a healing for Melissa."

The woman in the blue suit said, "I know!" Then she boldly walked up toward the altar where Melissa was standing and lovingly outstretched her hand, gently touching Melissa's tumors with the tips of her fingers. We were in awe. Melissa's tumors were impossible to detect from afar, especially in a darkened church. Nor had this stranger been told that Melissa even had cancer, much less what kind. The woman paused, and the room was filled with a warm silence. Melissa didn't move a muscle. We all held our breath.

As the woman laid her hand over Melissa's tumors, she said, "My granddaughter had the same thing at six months of age. She is now fourteen. You will be healed, too." She then removed her hand, looked into Melissa's eyes, and smiled. Melissa smiled back. The couple cheerfully bid everyone farewell and vanished from the church, departing as quickly and unexpectedly as they had arrived. (We are still looking for angel feathers!)

After the couple left, Father George began the healing ceremony, and when it was over we had lunch. Melissa was still so intrigued by the Celtic cross that Father George blessed one and gave it to her as a gift. It was a gift of remembrance and hope.

Several weeks after that healing, Melissa's mother called. This time she had wonderful news to share. The tumors were gone! The doctors were at a complete loss for how this could have happened. We had no explanation either, except that she had been blessed with a divine intervention. Today, Melissa is twenty-three years old. She is healthy and still finding God in her horses.

But the story does not end here. Several years after this incident, we moved to San Antonio. Deborah met a priest at a conference who was the one who supposedly had sent the couple from his parish in Monterey. However, the priest had never heard of either the man or the woman. In fact, he said he had never sent anyone to visit. He smiled at Deborah and said, "This isn't the first time."

At that moment we knew that communing with Trianero had given us the courage and open-mindedness to follow that high cross that the horse had shown Adele in her dream. We too felt very blessed, along with Melissa, for it was a reminder that the shadow of the Scottish wise man was hovering over us still.

Blocks in the Path

If we still had any doubts about horses being agents of grace, all uncertainty was erased at that moment. They have fulfilled their Celtic legacy by awakening the spiritual instinct in all of us. Since the beginning, they have served us, and the people who've worked with us, as messengers, angels, guides, matchmakers, merrymakers, and vigil holders. In very subtle ways they have always been there to push us in the right direction, particularly when we took the time to listen to and heed their clues. Truly, they have an uncanny ability to make the world go round, seeming to orchestrate situations and put the right people together at exactly the right time.

In spite of the guidance of our horses, and our own desire to learn from them, there have been times when we were less than successful in our efforts. Even then, however, some of the most difficult and heartbreaking lessons have provided us with insights that would benefit others who came into our lives.

One particular lesson turned out to be as valuable as it was tragic, for it revealed the potentially devastating consequences of ignoring or blocking our spiritual instincts. At one time or another, we all must address the negative or even destructive influences in our lives, and if we fail to do so directly, or fail to do so soon enough, it can have irrevocable consequences. We learned about this tragic story through a friend in the horse community.

Joy was a vivacious, beautiful, and beguiling young girl who was raised by an insanely jealous mother. Mrs. Byoot turned everything into a competition. If Joy sang one song, Mrs. Byoot sang five. The lesson that Joy learned from this was that Mama Byoot was never to be upstaged. She learned it was better to not develop her own gifts than to risk her mother's jealous rage.

Over time, Mrs. Byoot grew increasingly bitter. When Joy became a teenager, Mrs. Byoot berated, humiliated, condemned, and rejected her. Joy became increasingly depressed, even suicidal. Her grades in school dropped, and she withdrew emotionally.

Joy's father grew worried about her. Since Mr. Byoot knew his daughter loved horses, he believed that buying Joy a horse for Christmas might remedy what ailed her. Mr. Byoot was oblivious to how destructive his wife was to their daughter. He never imagined that his wife's competitiveness was the root of his daughter's problems.

Mr. Byoot bought the horse for Joy, and for a while his plan worked. Joy came out of her doldrums just as her father had hoped. From the moment Joy and her horse, Gray, set eyes on each other, they developed a deep compassion and love. At last, Joy had a friend of her own. Moreover, Joy's mother knew nothing about horses and so could not compete with her daughter over it.

Then one day Mrs. Byoot decided she wanted to ride Gray. Fearing her mother would get hurt, Joy tried to stop her, but her mother wouldn't listen. Mrs. Byoot mounted Gray, and the horse spun around, wheeled, and threw her to the ground. Mrs. Byoot was livid. She got to her feet and castigated her daughter for having such an ill-mannered horse. Joy felt responsible. A week later Mrs. Byoot insisted on riding again, and Gray repeated his hostile performance. He pinned his ears and bucked. Mrs. Byoot didn't fall, but it was sheer luck that kept her in the seat.

Fuming, Mrs. Byoot screamed for Joy to help her down. Then she picked up a stick and beat the horse mercilessly while Joy screamed at her mother to stop. When her mother finally stormed off, Joy broke down and wept. Gray hung his head on Joy's shoulder. Weeks passed, and then Joy's mother tried to ride again, incensed by the fact that the horse had defeated her. This time after falling, she kicked, screamed, and threw rocks at Gray. Finally, Mrs. Byoot gave up trying to ride.

Joy thought the worst was over. She and Gray could breathe again. They had won back their solitude. Joy began to ride Gray as before, with great pleasure and without incident. Meanwhile, unbeknownst to her, Mrs. Byoot secretly watched Joy and Gray from the kitchen window and nursed her toxic rage.

Joy's grades in school improved, and she decided that when she graduated from high school she was going to become a teacher. She was feeling hopeful and positive about life. One day, overjoyed because she had passed an English exam, she ran home to share the news with Gray. She flew to the barn to give the horse a big hug. Gray's stall was empty! Mrs. Byoot had sent him away. Joy was devastated.

Not even Mr. Byoot knew what Joy's mother had done with the horse, and she made it very clear that she would never tell and that Joy would never see Gray again. From that day forward, Joy's heart was filled with pain. Her friends said she never truly smiled again; she simply went through the motions of living. It was as if, with Gray's disappearance, Joy gave up on life. Many nights she cried herself to sleep, longing for the horse to be returned to her. Nobody in the family dared challenge Joy's mother, for they were all afraid of Mrs. Byoot's wrath.

Joy's life returned to the way it had been before Gray arrived, only it was worse, for she now knew she couldn't do anything without sparking her mother's jealousy. Joy graduated from high school, and though her grades were low, she went to college. Once she completed her education, she had a job waiting for her in Singapore. In a foreign country, perhaps she would at last be released from her mother's dark influences, and hopefully the tide would turn for her.

Many months after Joy had left, a mutual friend received a communiqué from Singapore. Joy was dead at thirty. It had all happened so suddenly, nobody had even known she was ill. Cancer was the diagnosis, but we have often wondered if she didn't die of a broken heart.

Joy had come into this world with natural grace, but her mother had done everything in her power to rob her of that gift and sever her from the spiritual instincts that fostered and nurtured her. Mrs. Byoot's destructive behavior was challenged only once — and not by her husband or by Joy, but by Joy's horse, Gray. And yet, while Gray had been the girl's only protector, he also became an object lesson in the fate that awaited anyone who actually stood up to Mrs. Byoot. If Gray had provided Joy an opportunity to challenge her mother, it was too late, for she was ill-equipped to take advantage of it. For Joy's entire life, Mrs. Byoot had systematically worked to stamp out her daughter's spirit. It had finally worked.

When we are severed from grace, by choice or by the sheer force of another's will, nothing seems to go right or move forward. It is during times like these that we need to rethink and change our way of handling life, no matter how painful change may seem. If we're unable to do so, as was the case with Joy, we can become irrevocably poisoned. At all times, we need to be very conscious of the quality of our relationships. And we must remember that, as adults, we always have a choice about the company we keep; we need not remain victims to the hurtful influence of another.

Our spiritual instinct gives us the wisdom to differentiate between friend and foe, and it is our best ally. It gives us the courage to stand up and be free, to remind ourselves and others that we belong only to God. Developing our spiritual instincts is really quite simple: every day, honor their sacredness, and regularly commune with other creatures that do the same, following the example of the Celts. This is easy to say, but it can take every ounce of one's will to accomplish. However, by so doing, we not only become a magnet for grace, but we immunize ourselves from all that is dark and toxic.

CHAPTER 10

The Contemplative Way

When we practice contemplation, the "puzzling reflections" of human limitation fade away. In the contemplative life the Celts and other mystics have described, it is as if we one day discover that the reality we've been seeing has been only a reflection in a mirror.

Divine silence is the contemplative way. Only in silence can you hear your own heart. What does it say? What does it know? Your heart guides you to the place where the soul resides, that deep, small voice that knows only to speak the truth. Your thoughts will quiet as you listen for this voice. Nature itself is within you; the kingdom is within. It is not dark, but light, and the light becomes brighter as you seek to know this territory. Within your heart, you connect the angels to this light.

Silence unites, whereas language often divides. The mystics were wise to know that language can cause divisiveness, because we often get stuck in our concepts and preconceived notions and fail to savor each experience anew. How often have fights been caused because we talked and explained too much?

Surrounded by nonstop noise, we forget that silence is the most expedient way to disengage the Ego and stop it from acting reflexively. By temporarily ceasing to talk, we stop our spinning mind machine and move to the heart. We gain access to unconscious inclinations. When the unconscious is made conscious, it is our greatest ally; left in darkness, the unconscious can overwhelm the entire personality. This awareness is what led St. Francis to tame and befriend the wolf. Today, we only associate him with birds, but he was the one who told us, Feed the wolf, and it will not devour you. Indeed, the wolf is our soul, and it needs to be nurtured, not overlooked. If it is ignored, it will become ravenous. Beware of the wolf in sheep's clothing, for this is a hungry wolf. Our soul parades as meek because we fear its fire. The wolf is our soul's fire, its passion, and its love for the Divine.

The contemplative way gives us the inner tools to stoke the fire and to foster a living relationship with the Divine. It is a simple method that teaches us to slow down, observe, and reflect. We learn to stand still in order to see the splendor in our midst and to remember what was original in nature before we made so many concessions to society. Through the contemplative life, we learn how to be reflective instead of reactive. Adopting this reflective stance is invaluable if we're to succeed in life, because it unleashes the power of love and diffuses anger and hate. This inner shift improves the quality of all our relationships. It even affects our business and professional affairs. It can change our chemistry, so that animals and birds no longer fear us.

CONTEMPLATIVE PRACTICES WITH HORSES

Today we run retreats and workshops called the Equine Experience™. These retreats help people to discover, remember, and live the Celtic Way of contemplation. The retreat is a five-day submersion into the world of horses. It is a chance for people to join a long line of equestrian pilgrims, dating back to antiquity. During this experience, participants discover a rich and meaningful heritage steeped in ancient, medieval, Renaissance, and Baroque traditions. The experience affords participants a time to reflect and discover their own souls. On retreat, participants learn to "re-collect" their spiritual faculties.

Hence, the Equine Experience is more than just a horse program; it is a venture for learning to love. Crossing this threshold from the mundane to the holy with a horse changes life perspectives and prepares humans to more effectively handle the graceful dance of surrender.

We stress developing a relationship with the horse, just as people in the past have done. Therefore, we introduce people to a deeper level of horse interplay, the silences and nuances of horse communication. Individuals learn to reach beyond human intellect and language, and begin to intuit what the horse is trying to say.

As riders move into silence and stillness with a horse, they learn to live in the presence of the One. To begin the process, however, humans need to learn to become *collected*. Becoming collected is the very thing equestrians ask horses to do when riding. To do so, people need to gain awareness, mindfulness, self-control, and sensitivity, which leads to inner and outer balance. They also need to lose their egocentric agendas.

We first teach people on horseback to open their chakras and the chakras of the horse by following rhythm, breath, and silence. We ask riders to simplify their communication, technique, and expectations. They should come to the horse empty, desiring only one thing, to join in Unity. When they do, they can move into a state of prayerful being. Only then can they meet creature to creature. Often they can first achieve this goal by doing nothing except breathing together. When people can reach progressive states of noninterference, the horse starts performing movements, even difficult ones, more harmoniously. When the rider becomes still in mind and body, she begins to sense and experience the horse in new and deeper ways. Communications with the horse or interventions then emerge from this attunement. When the actions of the rider grow from this silence, people learn to become reflective instead of impulsive or reactive, responsive instead of passive.

We also teach people to develop an extensive repertoire of communication while riding. Once they have learned some of the fundamentals of good equitation, balance, seat, position, and aids, riders are encouraged to enlarge their repertoire. They learn to adjust their timing to fit the needs of the horse. Often, quick, deliberate, and dramatic responses are necessary around horses. Quiet and still does not mean sluggish, unaware, or passive. Yet riders who are attuned to the horse speak through inner rhythms and invisible channels as well. Horses are innately in tune with the rhythm of nature and God's pulse, which is demonstrated as breath and heartbeat.

Increasing perceptiveness is aided through our program of special study, meditative practices, reflection, and awareness, as well as the natural process of struggle that accompanies all learning. Most horsemen of ancient times required apprentices to undergo a prolonged period of preparation. They were asked to observe, study, and even fast before they could ride a horse. Each apprentice was required to develop simple powers of observation. Without developing some of these basic and preliminary skills, horsemen and -women never acquire the building blocks of inner composure and calm. Nor do they develop the visionary powers necessary to create specific movements on horseback. Riding also requires visualization, sensitivity, heart power, intentionality, and confidence, not necessarily physical prowess.

Without inner composure and self-awareness, many people who ride remain fearful and don't know why. To feel in command on a horse, one must communicate with the horse, not simply sit on top. It is also necessary for a rider to know his or her own strengths and limitations. Voluntarily forgoing certain experiences on a horse that people know are beyond their present capability is just as important as doing everything themselves. Sitting on a horse, in our method, requires learning the basic skills of mind, body, and spirit.

SEEING FACE TO FACE

Henry Blake, an exceptional horsetrainer, shares a wonderful story about this contemplative way with horses. "Man's ability to be at one with the horse is also well illustrated by the story of the American slave who used to catch wild mustangs by going naked into the district where the herd of horses roamed, and live and move as a member of the herd. He would start off by approaching within two or three hundred yards of the herd and just stay there. When the horses moved, he moved with them. When they went to water, he went to water. When they grazed he would lie down beside the grazing herd. He would fetch his own food from a tree a mile or so away from the herd, where it was left for him. Within a fortnight or so he would be moving in amongst the wild horses and be accepted as a member of the herd. Then, when he had established his position he would half-drive, half-lead the mustangs into an already prepared corral. Simply by acting as a horse acted, thinking as a horse thought, behaving as a horse behaved, and having no contact with man, he gained the horses' trust and could single-handedly catch a complete herd of wild horses."[1] Isn't this similar to what St. Francis did with the wild animals?

This contemplative outlook teaches us to stay afloat when we encounter the inevitable dark and difficult undercurrents of life. Sometimes when we jump in or get swept up in these undercurrents, it can seem there is no outlet. When this happens, time-proven rituals and skills of the contemplative way can provide the staying power and courage we need to see the challenge through. In his book *Holy Longings,* Ronald Rolheiser says, "The rituals that sustain our daily lives do not work through novelty or by seeking to raise our psychic temperature. What they try to effect is not novelty, but rhythms, not currents but the timeless, and not the emotional but the archetypal."[2]

Contemplative practices have a wholly practical side, for they can help us see possibilities beyond our immediate reactions or impressions concerning a difficult situation. The reflective, open state of mind and heart that are developed on the contemplative path set the stage for fresh attitudes, deeper understanding, and insights. We suddenly have breakthroughs that allow us to see problems in a different light and that allow us to find answers and resolutions that seemed impossible only moments before. Eventually the skills of the contemplative way become second nature, fully integrated into our daily lives.

As calm unfolds, we are able to intuit something beyond the chaos.

Over the past few years, quantum physics and the most ancient contemplative practices have come to support each other in some rather amazing ways, suggesting that what mystics perceived, thousands of years ago, were truths embedded in the Cosmos itself. For example, both approach the issue of chaos and not-knowing in similar ways. Quantum physicists refer to chaos as the "fertile ground of transfiguration" or as "uncertainty." Similarly, the mystics often call it the "Cloud of Unknowing." Both physicist and mystic agree that beneath apparent chaos there is an implicit order. We may not be able to perceive that order immediately, but that does not mean it isn't there. To discover the implicit order, the mystic learns to see the world through God's eyes, developing a way of catching at least fleeting glimpses through a divine lens, cleared of the cloud of unknowing produced by our human lens. The New English Bible says, "Now we see only puzzling reflections in a mirror, but then we shall see face to face. My knowledge now is partial; then it will be whole, like God's knowledge of me" (I Corinthians 13:12–13).

When we practice contemplation, the "puzzling reflections" of human limitation fade away. In the contemplative life the Celts and other mystics have described, it is as if we one day discover that the reality we've been seeing has been only a reflection in a mirror. Then for a brief moment we turn away from the mirror and see the real thing. In that instant, all illusion fades away. This is the promise to those who follow the contemplative path: if we spend time with God, our Lover, this romance will insure new understanding and richness beyond the limits of human perception.

If we work toward this type of intimacy, seeing "face to face" instead of through the puzzling reflections of the mirror, our everyday lives with others, be they human or animal, start to move toward unification and Oneness. With clarity and stillness, our innate spiritual self emerges naturally and easily. This happens because we allow nature to lead the way. Since the ancients had great faith in the healing powers inherent in nature, they didn't hurry to try to resolve emotional upsets or find closure, as we do today. Instead, they had faith that emotional difficulties were mostly just puzzling reflections in the eyes of the beholder. These problems would resolve themselves as, perhaps in the next moment, the person would catch a glimpse of his or her problems through God's eyes. The ancients felt less pressure to force change; they felt more comfortable just observing what is.

J. Philip Newell, author and Celtic scholar, comments: "The story of the seventh day points to the restfulness of God. It is not opposed to the wild creative energies of the second day, but is the revealing of another dimension of God's creativity. The seven days of Genesis, as we have noted, are not a chronological account of the emergence of the universe in the past but a meditation on the ever-present mystery of creation. The life of creation is a theophany of God. It is a visible expression of the One who is essentially invisible, an intelligible sign of the One who is beyond knowledge. Just as the first day points to the light that is always at the heart of life, so the seventh reflects the stillness that is part of God's ongoing creativity."[3]

Through the simple act of meditation, of stilling our minds, we are moved into the silence that nurtures creativity. Those moments of quietude maximize our creativity, leading to highly productive and purposeful action. We now breathe new life because our full attention is momentarily turned to the Divine, where we see beyond the puzzling reflections of our own minds.

The mystics of all religions knew that it is only in silence that we can find our center. David Steindl-Rast writes the following about the mystical or contemplative tradition: "Not only is the mystical core of religion inexhaustible, it is also ultimately unspeakable. The heart of all ritual is stillness; the heart of all teaching is silence. The mystics of every tradition know this and keep telling us that *those who speak do not know, and those who know do not speak*."[4]

CHAPTER 11

Mystical Bonds of Friendship and Communion

Alleluia, the age-old expression of gratitude in communion, opens us to agape love, the recognition of our connection with all beings. To join together with other creatures in a song of joy moves us to experience the sacred in even the most mundane phenomena, transporting us from a self-centered way of being to a state in which we embrace, and are embraced by, all and everything. We shift from mere words to a prayerful expression of exultation, a chant of gratitude, if you will, resonating throughout eternity, crossing language, time, culture, and even species barriers.

W hen we go back in history two or three thousand years, we discover that the ideal of friendship once involved far more commitment than it does today. It was considered the most advanced form of intimacy. To be a friend was to be willing to lay down one's own life for another. This understanding gives Christ's words to his disciples — "I have called you friends" (John 15:15) — a very different perspective than is our understanding of friendship today. Similarly, as many historians have noted, Roman soldiers did not fight for their country; they fought for their friends. No one could qualify as a friend or lover who was not on your side. Over time, friendship evolved into "kinsman" or "blood brother," usually implying a strong relationship forged out of the experience of facing a common enemy or braving a dangerous venture together.

While most of us in modern times probably don't think of friendship as a life-or-death commitment, it is still recognized as a special relationship, certainly not one to be taken lightly. *The Oxford English Dictionary* describes friendship as "being joined with another in mutual beneficence and intimacy."

One often wonders if, through our long history together, the bonds between horses and humans are somehow borne within even our genes. All the qualities of friendship, even down to the commitment to lay down one's life for a friend, show up in the relationships established between horses and humans. We have had many such experiences that bear witness to this theory. In particular, there is one involving a stallion named José.

This gorgeous stallion was causing problems for his owners. José had little tolerance for people he didn't like. Every time someone he disliked passed by, he tried to bite him. José would rush to the stall door, stick his head out, open his mouth as wide as he could, and take a big hunk out of the individual. Seeing his entire set of teeth understandably scared a lot of people away. Since the barn had many visitors, he had become a menace.

Our friends, his owners, asked if he could come to our ranch. They were willing to try anything because he was such an exquisite stallion. We accepted, and José settled in beautifully. After three weeks he was not the same horse. He no longer tried to bite or terrify passersby. The three of us, and our ninety-six-year-old grandmother, adored this horse, and the relationship was mutual. We spent hours working and playing with him. José was a joy.

The depth of his love for us was revealed during a photo shoot for a magazine. The day of the shoot, José and his full brother Pepe, also a stallion, were aligned side by side. The owner's nephew was riding Pepe. Deborah was riding José. As they were standing quietly and waiting for the photographer to set up the shot, Pepe lunged sideways and attacked José's neck and head. Then Pepe reared and began striking José with his two front legs.

Pepe began pummeling José with his two front hooves, and Deborah was caught in between. Pepe's hooves flashed back and forth in front of Deborah's head, and as she remained straight in the saddle, the hooves grazed her left forehead. Everyone was watching, but there was nothing anyone could do. Finally, Deborah was able to slide down José's side onto the ground, out of the line of fire. José then defended himself, and the fight could be controlled.

What happened initially was remarkable. José never moved one inch. He remained as still as a statue. This kind of self-restraint is unusual for stallions because it goes against their survival instinct. After all, Pepe was seriously attacking him. Yet José's every move was calculated to protect his rider, even though it jeopardized his own well-being. He knew that if he attacked back, Deborah would be in serious trouble. He was right. The flashing hooves could have hit her head directly several times. As it was, the strikes near her eyes were so close that if José had defended himself, Deborah would have likely lost her left eye. Thankfully, José made no attempt to fight back until Deborah had rolled to safety. Everyone was momentarily silenced by José's noble and selfless gesture of friendship and love.

Fortunately, we were able to get the situation under control, and neither stallion was seriously harmed. José, however, had earned the title of faithful friend. He eventually went back to his owners and was given a fresh start. To this day, we cherish his memory and feel blessed to have had such a loyal and loving equine friend. He taught us about how communion ignites a true friendship.

We must be careful not to weigh down these most beautiful creatures with our selfish needs, particularly if we are to know them as our spiritual friends. Often without thinking, humans today use horses for therapy, burdening them with our troubles. When we come to horses only to dump our emotional problems on them, we are thinking only of ourselves, and we forget that friendship is about giving and receiving. When we expect the horse to carry our emotional baggage, we transform a noble and fine friend into a mundane beast of burden. Instead of reducing them to our level, we need to learn to fly with them, above the mundane and into transcendent realms.

As we read in Ecclesiastes: "Indeed, the fate of man and beast is identical; one dies, the other too, and both have the same breath; man has no advantage over the beast, for all is vanity. Both go to the same place; both originate from the dust and to the dust both return. Who knows if the spirit of man mounts upward or if the spirit of the beast goes down to the earth?" (3:19–21, Jerusalem Bible).

COMMUNION

When our mare Alicia gave us instructions to return to church to learn about communion, we were initially unsure what to do. Many who worked with us who had heard about Alicia's message asked whether we thought it necessary to go to a church to receive communion. We couldn't answer because we were struggling with that question ourselves. We were torn as to how to proceed, weighing the merit of doing our own thing, which we preferred, or participating in a formal tradition.

A memorable encounter at an annual horse conference in San Diego ignited more questions. It is also another example of the type of extraordinary events that began to occur as we deepened our relationship with horses.

Ironically, the encounter literally took place at a table, over food — the original reference point for communion. We were excited about finding an authentic Peruvian restaurant and had arrived for lunch. We were seated by a very cordial waiter, Philipe. The restaurant was empty, he was the only waiter in the house, and we began to converse briefly in Spanish. We learned that he himself was from Peru. When he saw the Celtic cross we had just bought, he became very excited.

Philipe enthusiastically launched into a discourse on the meaning of the Celtic cross in antiquity and how it had its roots in communion. Communion, as he described it, places each of us back into the cosmic circle of life, where there is no beginning or end, where we are on equal ground with all of life, and life is fluid. As an aficionado of Arthurian legend, he highlighted, "We also sit and dine at King Arthur's round table."

He explained that communion is a tradition that most people assume started with Christ; however, it is far more ancient. It goes back at least five thousand years, if not more, and provides a way we can heighten our communication with others in time and space, and even with those outside of our temporal dimensions. In other words, communion brings together the physical and the spiritual, the seen and unseen realities that affect all of our lives. While words may be used in the ritual of communion, the act reaches beyond verbal communication to love.

We were fascinated by this philosopher-waiter. We shared with him some of our adventures about spirituality and horses, and we told him about our Peruvian mare, Alicia. He responded with a huge smile.

He said, "Alicia wants you to talk with St. Francis, St.

Anthony, and others because they love animals. Your horses are directing you to some of the men and women in the early tradition whose wisdom is being forgotten. Communion gives you the ability to contact them. Joining together with others in one voice resurrects the sleeping souls you may need. Many people today don't realize it, but we are not alone. There are invisible resources available that are right at our fingertips if we unite and call sincerely."

Philipe's thoughts dovetailed with the theories of scientist Rupert Sheldrake, whose intriguing ideas about communion we had recently encountered. Dr. Sheldrake says, "The purpose of ritual is to connect the present participants with the original event that the ritual commemorates and also link them with all those who have participated in the ritual in the past. Ritual is something to do with crossing time, annihilating distance in time, bringing the past into the present. The Christian Holy Communion, for example, re-creates or connects participants with the original Last Supper and also connects them with those who have participated since; it brings them into a connection with what is called the Communion of Saints."[1]

Dr. Sheldrake emphasizes, "From a secular, rationalist point of view, none of this makes sense. Ritual is just one example of superstition to which human beings are unfortunately prone, until these irrational hangovers from the past can be eradicated by enlightened education. But rituals are remarkably persistent, even in secular societies. People seem to have a need for them, and when deprived of traditional ones, they re-create their own. Gangs, for example, often re-create initiation rituals, having been deprived of socially approved rites of passage."[2]

We sat in the restaurant with Philipe for four hours or more listening to him talk, fascinated by the parallels between what he was saying, what Sheldrake says, and our own experiences.

Philipe insisted that this message from our horse was not intended just for us but for the whole planet. He spoke of how communion helps us transcend our human limitations. It is a way to unify the consciousness of a community, to give us a stronger voice. By uniting our hearts in the sacred relationship of communion, we act in alignment with the original design of the universe, which is to love.

Out of curiosity, we asked Philipe what he did in Peru. We speculated that he had a degree in science or medicine. He was amused by our suggestion that he was a doctor. With a twinkle in his eye, he lovingly answered that he had an advanced degree in nutrition.

As all good things must, that pleasant afternoon of great company and stimulating talk and insight came to an end. It had been a memorable day. We had enjoyed fine food and a stirring conversation, and there were no crowds. We thanked Philipe, left the restaurant, and felt absolutely refreshed.

Because we had had such a good time, we decided to go back to the same restaurant the next day for lunch. Upon our arrival, we asked the owner for Philipe. She stared at us with a puzzled expression. She thought we must be lost. The restaurant was full, and there were several waiters around, but no Philipe. When we insisted that we'd eaten there the day before, and that our waiter had been a man named Philipe, she just shook her head. "I'm sorry," she said, "but we don't have anyone by that name working here. We never have had, I am very sure. You must be mistaken."

We felt more than a little ridiculous. Surely we hadn't dreamed our lunch with Philipe! Was this the hovering of the Scottish shaman?

It took months to digest this experience. We could not stop thinking about that afternoon with Philipe and the ideas we'd exchanged; without a doubt, we could not deny that it had happened. It was as a result of this encounter that we started taking a closer look at the meaning and purpose of communion.

The Cosmic Community

In its most essential form, communion creates a line of communication with the spiritual dimension. It teaches us a special language of the heart. It is the same language we speak with the horses, one in which we refrain from doubt, begging, and pleading. Instead, we affirm and give thanks, accepting the already present gift of love. This grateful stance liberates our energy and binds us to beings and situations with which the Divine wants us to unite, not for personal gain or egocentric satisfaction but for something much larger than that.

Communion is a coming together in celebration. It can include a ritual, an attitude, and an ideal way of conducting our lives. Though it is frequently considered a Christian practice, it is not exclusive to any one religion, sect, or spiritual practice. In fact, it is a universal phenomenon, perhaps best understood as an immersion in the sacred. We give thanks and remember the Deity. That's communion, most certainly. Communion can be group-oriented or individualized. Communion is the ultimate expression of spiritual love, which joins us all as one.

Alleluia, the age-old expression of gratitude in communion, opens us to *agape love,* the recognition of our connection with all beings. To join together with other creatures in a song of joy moves us to experience the sacred in even the most mundane phenomena, transporting us from a self-centered way of being to a state in which we embrace, and are embraced by, all and everything. We shift from mere words to a prayerful expression of exultation, a chant of gratitude, if you will, resonating throughout eternity, crossing language, time, culture, and even species barriers.

Agape is the deepest form of communication because we are not the givers but the recipients. We do not ask for something specific from God, as in a typical petitionary prayer; rather, we receive God. We open ourselves and God penetrates. This opening requires faith and trust. As a matter of fact, since communion occurs in silence, we relinquish our control and stop telling God what we need. The Omnipotent One can make those decisions on our behalf.

Communion, which derives from the word *commune,* is one of the most important rituals in the contemplative traditions. It is important because it is a reenactment of being in a state of perfect Oneness. It epitomizes all that the mystic hopes to achieve.

We are emptied of our human will and infused with divine strength and power, giving God an opportunity to fill us with a new kind of nourishment. Through love, we leave the secular and sojourn with our Beloved. It is a mysterious practice because it permits God to dwell not only outside but within us.

By consistently practicing communion, we allow each one of our cells to be touched. Every part of our being is bathed in this love by a process of intermingling. We are progressively changed by a process we can neither comprehend nor control. Consequently, the limited *I* is enveloped by the *Only I AM.* It is here that we find strength and courage, joined with our own inner divinity. Additionally, communion always involves community because our relationship with God never remains self-serving; it always turns toward others.

Communion brings us into contact with the universal information fields that Dr. Sheldrake calls morphic resonance. Dr. Sheldrake comments, "From the point of view of *morphic resonance,* rituals make perfect sense. By consciously performing ritual acts in as similar a way as possible to the way they have been done before, the participants enter into morphic resonance with those who have carried out the ritual in the past. There is a collapse of time. There is an invisible presence of all those who have done the ritual before, a transtemporal ritual community."[3]

AN ANCIENT RITUAL

The ancients have known about the power of giving praise. Quantum scientists have also done recent studies that substantiate the might of unifying our voices and channeling our minds in one direction. Consciousness can literally change matter when people join together and channel their intentions. It involves elements of sacrifice, feeding, recollection, and merging with the Divine.

Communion is not limited to the act of drinking wine and eating bread. It should also occur in our everyday experiences. As Father Steindl-Rast writes, "Religious experience is simply our awareness of communion with the Ultimate.... Communion with the Ultimate may surprise and overwhelm us unawares in peak moments of aliveness — on horseback, on a mountaintop, on the prow of a ship, under the dome of the night sky, or in a lover's arms."[4]

We have discovered that the actual ritual of taking communion jump-starts our spiritual system. On retreats, daily communion with the horses makes for richness and fulfills our spiritual need.

THE HISTORIC ROOTS OF COMMUNION

Early civilizations always paid homage to the Divine. Some believed that to fail in this might bring death. The Aztecs, for example, had an annual human sacrifice as an offering to the Sun God. This was done in hopes of appeasing the Divine. They feared that if they did not pay their respects, the sun would stop rising.

According to ancient wisdom, to stay in communication was an act of true intimacy. As British mystic Evelyn Underhill states, "We know a thing by uniting with it, by assimilating it, by interpenetration of it and ourselves. It gives itself to us in so far as we give ourselves to it; and it is because our outflow towards things is usually so perfunctory and so languid that our comprehension of things is so perfunctory and languid too."[5]

As the Christian religion developed, bread and wine were integrated into rituals of communion to symbolize the sacrificing of our own selfish needs and desires and sharing that sacrifice with others in a kind of mutual act of sacrifice and nurture that honored God's plan. Theodore Thass-Thienemann writes, "This elementary philosophy of kinship was represented primarily by the common sacrifice and the sharing of the sacrificial meal. In further expression its manifestation became any eating or drinking together. The same food absorbed in two persons establishes unity especially if this food carries the meaning of spiritual incorporation and is supposed to be accepted at the same time by the spirit....

"The kinship in blood was once the only criterion of *friendship*. One can even observe that kinship had the decisive part in the development of *love*. No man could exist alone in the desert. The only ones whom he could trust were his own kin. He expanded the generic kinship to those with whom he was united by a blood covenant, they became his *brothers* or *friends*."[6]

Since we submit ourselves to the transformational power of the mystery, communion requires nothing of us except conscious, dedicated, and regular participation. Thus we will be transformed from the inside out.

Furthermore, to *remember* means literally "to bring the body together," to re-member it. It means to become whole, to work together, to become unified in the most powerful force available, the spirit of love. In the book *The Medium, the Mystic and the Physicist,* author Lawrence LeShan maintains, "The recurring theme *God is Love* appears to mean exactly what it says; that there is a force, an energy, that binds the cosmos together and moves always in the direction of its harmonious action and the fruition of the separate connected parts. In man, this force emerges and expresses itself as love, and this is the *spark of the divine* in each of us."[7]

In the symbolic act of eating together, we are acknowledging and accepting our birthright. We are attending the lavish banquet to which we have all been invited. We are savoring the food, enjoying the music, and loving the company. Through communion we get glimmers of an invisible kingdom. When we unite in love, we are participating in the sacredness of life. Communion becomes more than a ritual; it becomes a way of life. God's plan is expressed through our minds, bodies, hands, hearts, and works, and made visible in the world through our very presence.

Since we humans are incapable of understanding this ineffable reality, we simply have to get down on our knees in reverence and bow. We will never understand divine intelligence and wisdom with our own individual minds. The only place our individual minds and the Divine Mind can meld is in our hearts. Since our heart of hearts belongs to God, it is a private and silent rendezvous. Communion is an unceasing prayer of the heart, and our only transport into this unseen world. We travel to this invisible place in silence, reminiscent of our nonverbal beginnings. Momentarily, we cease our excessive dependency on meaningless and empty words.

Epilogue

Experiences such as these — igniting revelation and epiphany — often come at the most unexpected and even mundane moments in our lives. And yet, in their own way they affirm our connections with the Divine.

Several months after completing this book, Adele was visiting Mexico City when she was approached by a stranger at the Main Cathedral. This middle-aged man walked over to Adele and asked to be her guide. She hadn't considered having a guide, but when he said, "Please just give me twenty minutes," she conceded.

As they meandered through the architectural wonder that is the Main Cathedral, Adele found her guide's words and message compelling. He spoke about the meaning of communion, the mystery of the saints, the significance of altars and angels. The guide whispered, "The archangel Michael is a warrior saint, and is always here to protect us if we call upon him.

At the first sound of our voice Michael will come blazing out of the sun."

Adele thought it strange that he would talk about St. Michael, the Celtic saint of the horses. She listened intently to this man's soft-spoken voice. There was something very familiar about him. It was as if she already knew him. Yet, even though he spoke perfect English, he explained that he had never set foot outside of Mexico. Adele was overcome by an odd sense of love in his presence. She wondered why he had singled her out of the crowd, and where she had heard these words he was speaking to her.

As they strolled, he spoke about *hermeticism* — the study of the unseen dimensions of reality — and humanity. He continued, "All healing comes from the spirit. If you wish to know God, you must immerse yourselves in nature, spend hours contemplating a flower or an animal. Your heart will open to the unseen world."

Adele thought it odd that a cathedral guide was focusing so much attention on these obscure and rather esoteric matters. Certainly these subjects were not what most tourists seeking a tour of the cathedral would have been wanting to hear. Other guides were talking about the Pope's most recent visit to this place, an event of historical significance, and about the cardinal presiding that day at Mass. Adele's guide talked only about mysticism and about religious subjects that delved deeply into the mystery. Then it hit her! Adele remembered the voice of our Peruvian waiter and the eyes of the Scottish shepherd from so many years ago — two old friends who had made such an important impact on our lives.

As her tour of the cathedral came to a close, the guide turned to her and said, "As a student of human nature, you already know many of these things. Keep going. Go deeper. The whole of reality is invisible, and those of us who know it are connected in a cosmic brotherhood. We always recognize each other."

As the man walked away, he faded into the blinding sun. In that moment, Alicia, our golden mare, came to Adele's mind, reminding her of what it is like to move beyond the everyday reality of the senses into the reality of the invisible. Like the Golden Mare, this guide, as well as the Scottish shepherd and the mysterious waiter, came into our lives, seemingly out of the blue, to reaffirm for us the importance of this work.

Experiences such as these — igniting revelation and epiphany — often come at the most unexpected and even mundane moments in our lives. And yet, in their own way they affirm our connections with the Divine. In the kind of work we've been exploring in this book, it can be difficult to find confirmation in the everyday world. Moments such as this therefore take on a depth of meaning and purpose, reminding us that the material plane is not the main show but only a fragment of a much larger reality.

Notes

Introduction

1. J. Krishnamurti, *The Flame of Attention* (San Francisco: HarperSanFrancisco, 1984), 24–25.
2. Henry Corbin, *Creative Imagination in the Sufism of Ibn' Arabi*, trans. Ralph Manheim, Bollingen Series XCI (Princeton, NJ: Princeton University Press, 1969), 247.

Chapter 2:
The Wisdom of the Iberian Horse Community

1. Elana Maria Whitshaw, *Atlantis in Spain* (Stelle, IL: Adventures Unlimited Press, 1994), 248.
2. *Time Frame 1500–600 B.C.*, *Barbarian Tides* (Alexandria, VA: Time-Life Books, 1987), 69.
3. Theodore Thass-Thienemann, *The Interpretation of Language: Understanding the Unconscious Meaning of Language*, vol. 2 (New York: Jason Aronson, 1968), 266.
4. This quote from the Koran is from *The Literate Horse Calendar 2000* (San Francisco: Browntrout Publishing, 1999).

CHAPTER 3:
ANIMALS AWAKENING THE HUMAN SOUL

1. Andrew Harvey, *The Essential Mystics: The Soul's Journey into Truth* (Edison, NJ: Castle Books, 1998), 120.

2. Jacob Needleman, *Lost Christianity: A Journey of Rediscovery to the Centre of Christian Experience* (1980; repr., Rockport, MA: Element, 1993), 152; italics added.

3. Needleman, *Lost Christianity*, 175.

4. Ravi Ravindra, *Christ the Yogi: A Hindu Reflection on the Gospel of John* (Rochester, VT: Inner Traditions, 1990), 14.

5. Needleman, *Lost Christianity*, 156.

6. John Scotus Eriugena, *The Voice of the Eagle, the Heart of Celtic Christianity: Homily on the Prologue to the Gospel of St. John*, trans. Christopher Bamford (New York: Lindisfarne Press, 1990), 69.

7. Stanislav Grof and Christina Grof, eds., *Spiritual Emergency: When Personal Transformation Becomes a Crisis* (New York: J. P. Tarcher, 1989).

CHAPTER 4:
MYSTICISM AND HORSES — AN ANCIENT WAY OF BEING

1. Personal correspondence from Marcia Zukowski.

CHAPTER 5:
THE CELTIC WAY —
A MODEL FOR SPIRITUAL CROSS-TRAINING

1. John Scotus Eriugena, *The Voice of the Eagle, the Heart of Celtic Christianity: Homily on the Prologue to the Gospel of St. John*, trans. Christopher Bamford (New York: Lindisfarne Press, 1990), 82.

2. J. Philip Newell, *The Book of Creation: An Introduction to Celtic Spirituality* (New York: Paulist Press, 1999), 27.

3. Newell, *The Book of Creation,* 27.
4. Newell, *The Book of Creation,* 26–27.
5. Prudence Jones and Nigel Pennick, *A History of Pagan Europe* (New York: Barnes & Noble Books, 1995), 86.
6. Newell, *The Book of Creation,* 22.

Chapter 6:
Celtic Mysticism

1. Robert Van de Weyer, introduction to *The Letters of Pelagius: Celtic Soul Friend,* ed. Robert Van de Weye (Evesham, England: Arthur James, 1995), ii.
2. Newell, *The Book of Creation,* 67–68.
3. John Marsden, *The Illustrated Bede,* trans. John Gregory (London: Macmillan, 1996), 134–35.
4. Marsden, *The Illustrated Bede,* 154.
5. Nigel Pennick, *The Celtic Saints: An Illustrated and Authoritative Guide to These Extraordinary Men and Women* (New York: Sterling Publishing, 1997), 91.
6. Marsden, *The Illustrated Bede,* 144.
7. John O'Donohue, *Anam Cara: A Book of Celtic Wisdom* (New York: HarperCollins, 1997), 226.
8. Thomas Merton, *Contemplative Prayer* (New York: Doubleday, 1969), 38–39.
9. Murat Yagan, *I Come from Behind Kaf Mountain: A Spiritual Autobiography of Murat Yagan,* ed. Patricia Johnston and Joan McIntyre (Vernon, B.C.: Kebzeh Publications, 1997), 157.

Chapter 7:
Living Close to the Vine

1. Evelyn Underhill, *Practical Mysticism: A Little Book for Normal People* (Guildford, England: Eagle, 1991), 42.
2. Bamford, *The Voice of the Eagle,* 109.
3. Bamford, *The Voice of the Eagle,* 109.

CHAPTER 8:
DROPPING OUR ILLUSIONS

1. Wayne Teasdale, *The Mystic Heart: Discovering a Universal Spirituality in the World's Religions* (Novato, CA: New World Library, 1999), 178.

CHAPTER 9:
THE SPIRITUAL INSTINCT

1. J. E. Cirlot, *A Dictionary of Symbols,* trans. Jack Sage (New York: Philosophical Library, Vail-Ballou Press, 1962), xxvi.
2. Alan Riding, "Matisse: From the Secular to the Divine," *New York Times,* June 5, 2001.
3. Joseph T. Shipley, *Dictionary of Word Origins* (New York: Philosophical Library, 1945), 308.

CHAPTER 10:
THE CONTEMPLATIVE WAY

1. Henry Blake, *Talking with Horses: A Study of Communication between Man and His Horse* (North Pomfret, VT: Trafalgar Square Publishing, 1990), 95.
2. Ronald Rolheiser, *Holy Longings: The Search for a Christian Spirituality* (New York: Doubleday, 1999), 236.
3. Newell, *The Book of Creation,* 101.
4. David Steindl-Rast, foreword to *Meister Eckhart, from Whom God Hid Nothing: Sermons, Writings and Sayings,* ed. David O'Neal (Boston and London: Shambhala, 1996), ix.

CHAPTER 11:
MYSTICAL BONDS OF FRIENDSHIP AND COMMUNION

1. Mathew Fox and Rupert Sheldrake, *Natural Grace: Dialogues on Creation, Darkness and the Soul in Spirituality and Science* (New York: Doubleday, 1996), 168.

2. Fox and Sheldrake, *Natural Grace,* 166–67.

3. Fox and Sheldrake, *Natural Grace,* 167.

4. David Steindl-Rast, foreword to O'Neal, *Meister Eckhart,* vii–viii.

5. Underhill, *Practical Mysticism,* 2–3.

6. Thass-Thienemann, *The Interpretation of Language,* 317–18.

7. Lawrence LeShan, *The Medium, the Mystic and the Physicist: Toward a General Theory of the Paranormal* (New York: Penguin Arkana, 1966), 166–67.

Bibliography

Blake, Henry. *Talking with Horses: A Study of Communication between Man and His Horse.* North Pomfret, VT: Trafalgar Square Publishing, 1990.

Carmicheal, Alexander. *Carmina Gadelica: Hymns and Incantations Collected in the Highlands and Islands of Scotland in the Last Century.* Edinburg: Floris Books, 1997. First published 1992 by Lindisfarne Press (Great Britain).

Cassian, John. *John Cassian: Conferences.* Translated by Colm Luibheid. Mahwah, NJ: Paulist Press, 1985.

Cirlot, J. E. *A Dictionary of Symbols.* Translated by Jack Sage. New York: Philosophical Library, Vail-Ballou Press, 1962.

Corbin, Henry. *Creative Imagination in the Sufism of Ibn' Arabi.* Translated from the French by Ralph Manheim. Bollingen Series XCI. Princeton, NJ: Princeton University Press, 1969.

Cordeiro, Arsenio Raposo. *Lusitano Horse: Son of the Wind.* Lisbon: Edicoes INAPA, 1991.

Cunliffe, Barry. *The Celtic World.* New York: McGraw Hill, 1979.

Dossey, Larry. *Healing Words: The Power of Prayer and the Practice of Medicine.* San Francisco: HarperCollins, 1997.

————. *Prayer Is Good Medicine: How to Reap the Healing Benefits of Prayer.* San Francisco: HarperSanFrancisco, 1993.

Duncan, Anthony. *The Elements of Celtic Christianity.* Rockport, MA: Element, 1992.

————. *The Sword in the Sun: Dialogue with an Angel.* Albuquerque, NM: Sun Chalice Books, 1997.

Eriugena, John Scotus. *The Voice of the Eagle, the Heart of Celtic Christianity: Homily on the Prologue to the Gospel of St. John.* Translated and with an introduction by Christopher Bamford. New York: Lindisfarne Press, 1990.

Fox, Mathew. *Breakthrough: Meister Eckhart's Creation Spirituality in New Translation.* New York: Doubleday, 1980.

Fox, Mathew, and Rupert Sheldrake. *Natural Grace: Dialogues on Creation, Darkness and the Soul in Spirituality and Science.* New York: Doubleday, 1996.

Fraser, Andrew F. *The Native Horses of Scotland: Scottish Breeds of Horses and Their Folk.* Edinburgh: John Donald Publishers, 1987.

Godwin, Malcolm. *The Holy Grail: Its Origins, Secrets and Meaning Revealed.* New York: Penguin Studio, 1994.

Grof, Stanislav, and Christina Grof, eds., *Spiritual Emergency: When Personal Transformation Becomes a Crisis.* New York: J. P. Tarcher, 1989.

Gueriniere, Francois Robichon de la. *School of Horsemanship.* Translated by Tracy Boucher. London: J. A. Allen & Company, 1994.

Harvey, Andrew. *The Essential Mystics: The Soul's Journey into Truth.* Edison, NJ: Castle Books, 1998.

Jones, Prudence, and Nigel Pennick. *A History of Pagan Europe.* New York: Barnes & Noble Books, 1995.

Joyce, Timothy. *Celtic Christianity: A Sacred Tradition Vision of Hope.* Maryknoll, NY: Orbis Books, 1998.

Jung, Carl G. *Modern Man in Search of a Soul.* New York: Harcourt Brace & Company, 1933.

Keating, Thomas. *Intimacy with God*. New York: Crossroads Publishing Company, 1994.

———. *Open Heart, Open Mind: The Contemplative Dimension of the Gospel*. New York: Continuum Publishing Company, 1986.

Krishnamurti, J. *The Flame of Attention*. San Francisco: HarperSanFrancisco, 1984.

Leloup, Jean-Yves, trans. *The Gospel of Mary Magdalene*. Translated into English by Joseph Rowe. Rochester, VT: Inner Traditions International, 2002.

LeShan, Lawrence. *The Medium, the Mystic and the Physicist: Toward a General Theory of the Paranormal*. Middlesex, England: Penguin Arkana, 1966.

Llamas, Juan. *This Is the Spanish Horse*. Translated by Jane Rabagliat. London: J. A. Allen & Company, 1997.

Loch, Sylvia. *The Classical Rider: Being at One with Your Horse*. North Pomfret, VT: Trafalgar Square Publishing, 1997.

———. *The Royal Horse of Europe: The Story of the Andalusian and Lusitano*. London: J. A. Allen & Company, 1986.

Markdale, Jean. *The Celts: Uncovering the Mythic and Historic Origins of Western Culture*. 1976. Reprint, Rochester, VT: Inner Traditions International, 1993.

Marsden, John. *The Illustrated Bede*. Translated by John Gregory. London: Macmillan, 1996.

McCormick, Adele. "History of the Peruvian Paso Horse," *Nuestro Caballo* magazine, January 1997, April 1997.

McGinn, Bernard. *The Flowering of Mysticism: Men and Women in the New Mysticism 1200–1350*. New York: Crossroads Publishing Company, 1998.

———. *The Foundations of Mysticism: Origins to the Fifth Century*. New York: Crossroads Publishing Company, 1995.

———. *The Growth of Mysticism: Gregory the Great through the 12th Century*. New York: Crossroads Publishing Company, 1996.

Merton, Thomas. *Contemplative Prayer.* New York: Doubleday, 1969.

———. *New Seeds of Contemplation.* 1961. Reprint, New York:
  New Directions, 1972.

———. *The Wisdom of the Desert: Sayings from the Desert
  Fathers of the Fourth Century.* 1960. Reprint, New York:
  New Directions, 1970.

Morgan, Morris H., ed. *Xenophon: The Art of Horsemanship.*
  1962. Reprint, London: J. A. Allen, 1984.

Needleman, Jacob. *Lost Christianity: A Journey of Rediscovery
  to the Centre of Christian Experience.* 1980. Reprint, Rockport, MA: Element, 1993.

Newell, J. Philip. *The Book of Creation: An Introduction to
  Celtic Spirituality.* New York: Paulist Press, 1999.

———. *Listening for the Heartbeat of God: A Celtic Spirituality.* Mahwah, NJ: Paulist Press, 1997.

Nicolas, Antonio T. de, trans. *St. John of the Cross (San Juan de
  la Cruz), Alchemist of the Soul: His Life, His Poetry (Bilin-
  gual), His Prose.* York Beach, ME: Samuel Weiser, 1996.

Nouwen, Henri J. M. *The Way of the Heart: Desert Spirituality
  and Contemporary Ministry.* San Francisco: HarperSan-
  Francisco, 1981.

O'Donohue, John. *Anam Cara: A Book of Celtic Wisdom.* New
  York: HarperCollins, 1997.

Oliveira, Nuno. *Reflections on Equestrian Art.* Translated by
  Phyllis Field. London: J. A. Allen & Company, 1976.

O'Loughlin, Thomas. *Celtic Spirituality.* Translated and introduced by Oliver Davies with the collaboration of Thomas
  O'Loughlin. Mahwah, NJ: Paulist Press, 1999.

O'Neal, David, ed. *Meister Eckhart, from Whom God Hid
  Nothing: Sermons, Writings and Sayings.* Boston and London: Shambhala, 1996.

Palmer, Martin. *Living Christianity.* Rockport, MA: Element, 1993.

Pearsall, Paul. *The Heart's Code: Tapping the Wisdom and Power of Our Heart Energy.* New York: Broadway Books, 1998.

Pennick, Nigel. *The Celtic Saints: An Illustrated and Authoritative Guide to These Extraordinary Men and Women.* New York: Sterling Publishing, 1997.

Pussey, Edward, trans. *The Confessions of Saint Augustine.* New York: Collier Books, 1961.

Ravindra, Ravi. *Christ the Yogi: A Hindu Reflection on the Gospel of John.* Rochester, VT: Inner Traditions, 1990.

Rees, B. R. *Pelagius: Life and Letters.* Woodbridge, England: Boydell Press, 1991.

Riding, Alan. "Matisse: From the Secular to the Divine," *New York Times,* June 5, 2001.

Rolheiser, Ronald. *Holy Longings: The Search for a Christian Spirituality.* New York: Doubleday, 1999.

Shah, Indries. *The Way of the Sufi.* New York: E. P. Dutton & Co., 1968.

Sheldrake, Rupert. *Dogs That Know When Their Owners Are Coming Home: And Other Unexplained Powers of Animals.* New York: Crown, 1999.

———. *The Sense of Being Stared At: And Other Aspects of the Extended Mind.* New York: Crown, 2003.

Shipley, Joseph T. *Dictionary of Word Origins.* New York: Philosophical Library, 1945.

Teasdale, Wayne. *The Mystic Heart: Discovering a Universal Spirituality in the World's Religions.* Novato, CA: New World Library, 1999.

Thass-Thienemann, Theodore. *The Interpretation of Language: Understanding the Unconscious Meaning of Language.* Vol. 2. New York: Jason Aronson, 1968.

Time-Life Books. *Time Frame 1500–600 B.C.: Barbarian Tides.* Alexandria, VA: Time-Life Books, 1987.

Underhill, Evelyn. *Practical Mysticism: A Little Book for Normal People.* Guildford, England: Eagle, 1991.

Van de Weyer, Robert, ed. *The Letters of Pelagius: Celtic Soul Friend.* Evesham, England: Arthur James, 1995.

Walsh, James, ed. *The Cloud of Unknowing.* Ramsey, NJ: Paulist Press, 1981.

Whitshaw, Elana Maria. *Atlantis in Spain.* Stelle, IL: Adventures Unlimited Press, 1994. Originally published as *Atlantis in Andalucia* (London: Rider & Company, 1928).

Woods, Richard. *The Spirituality of the Celtic Saints.* Maryknoll, NY: Orbis Books, 2000.

Yagan, Murat. *I Come from Behind Kaf Mountain: A Spiritual Autobiography of Murat Yagan.* Ed. Patricia Johnston and Joan McIntyre. Vernon, B.C.: Kebzeh Publications, 1997.

Index

About the Authors

Adele von Rüst McCormick, Ph.D., Marlena Deborah McCormick, Ph.D., and Thomas E. McCormick, M.D., have been psychotherapists for a span of over forty years, designing and running a series of unique and innovative programs using horses to help people with mental illness, criminals, and individuals with drug and alcohol addiction. Currently they are the codirectors of the Institute for Conscious Awareness and cofounders of the Hacienda Tres Aguilas Ltd. Equine Experience Programs™ in San Antonio, Texas, which offers courses and retreats using ancient principles and practices of kinship with horses to develop human spirituality and intuition. Adele and Marlena are authors of the book *Horse Sense and the Human Heart: What Horses Can Teach Us about Trust, Bonding, Creativity, and Spirituality.*

Marlena Deborah McCormick holds a Ph.D. in psychology. She has worked in a variety of traditional clinical settings and in private practice in the San Francisco Bay Area. She is an accomplished equestrian, studying classical Spanish dressage with international masters.

A psychotherapist for over forty years, Adele von Rüst McCormick, Ph.D., has also been founder of several treatment residences for psychotic adults and adolescents. She has been a consultant to Stanford Hospital, Belmont Hills Hospital, Presbyterian Hospital, Agnews State Hospital, and the U.S. government, along with a variety of other organizations, over the last forty years.

Dr. Thomas E. McCormick began his medical career in general practice and through this experience became even more intrigued by the mind/body connection, which eventually led to a residency in psychiatry and four decades in private psychiatric practice. He did cutting-edge training in psychiatric emergency medicine at San Francisco General, a hospital serving the violent and indigent. He also taught at the University of California, San Francisco; the University of Madrid; and the University of Seville.

To contact the McCormicks, please write to:

Hacienda Tres Aguilas, Ltd.
Institute for Conscious Awareness
20475 Hwy. 46 W., Suite 180, #429
Spring Branch, TX 78070
(830) 438-2816
E-mail: thomasm@gvtc.com
Website: www.therapyhorsesandhealing.com